To Mike;
   Thanks for doing such a
great job in Sunday School.
yours for growth,
Gary Harney

100 Great Growth Ideas

100 GREAT GROWTH IDEAS

NEIL E. JACKSON, JR.

BROADMAN PRESS
NASHVILLE, TENNESSEE

ISBN: 0-8054-5085-8
Dewey Decimal Classification: 268.1
Subject Headings: SUNDAY SCHOOLS—ADMINISTRATION //
CHURCH GROWTH
Library of Congress Catalog Card Number: 89-37087

Printed in the United States of America

Library of Congress Cataloging-in-Publication Data

Jackson, Neil E., Jr.
    100 great growth ideas / Neil E. Jackson, Jr.
      p.   cm.
    ISBN 0-8054-5085-8
    1. Sunday-schools—Growth. I. Title. II. Title: One hundred
great growth ideas.
BV1523.G75J33   1990
268—dc20   89-37087
                                         CIP

Foreword

Neil Jackson has done it again! From his vast array of experience with churches and people, he has put together another creative and practical book: *100 Great Growth Ideas*.

In concept and content, the book has a disarming, down-to-earth simplicity. These growth ideas are from people who have tried them. They have worked and have been useful. You will find effective help close at hand in this book.

These one hundred ideas are organized under topics like motivation, prospects, visitation, enrollment, high attendance day, worker appreciation, and equipping the saints.

In short, there is something here for everyone who is interested in doing a more effective work in their church. Pastor, minister of education, Sunday School director, and other leaders—try this book. I believe you'll like the result you obtain from using these ideas.

Harry M. Piland, Director
Sunday School Division
The Sunday School Board
    of the Southern Baptist Convention

Preface

There are many sharp, creative evangelistic leaders across the nation. The Lord has blessed us with these. They serve churches in the role of pastors, ministers of education and youth, children's workers, Sunday School directors, state leaders, directors of missions, denominational officials, teachers, and laypersons.

This book is a collection of 100 growth ideas that work. All contributors have used the ideas successfully in their own churches. This book is dedicated to them.

The ideas that follow are short, simple, and successful. Each idea has the name of the contributor and the contributor's church. The list of contributors is in the back of the book. If an idea does not identify a contributor, the idea was created by the author.

Blessings on you as you continue to reach people for Christ and His glory.

NEJ

Contents

day School Teacher   95. Letters of Appreciation   96. We
Appreciate You   97. February: Love Month   98. Member
Appreciation Day   99. Highlighting the Worker
100. The Golden Key Award

100 Great Growth Ideas

1
Motivation Ideas
for Growth

1. Lead for Input

When persons give input, they have already committed themselves. For in essence, they are saying, "Here is a way you can do the job, a way I would like to make things happen—a way I wouldn't mind spending my time and energy."

As a leader, you want to unite the "forces." Forces are the people and resources which have the greatest possible impact toward reaching your desired goal(s). Draw heavily upon your "forces."

People are the executors of whatever you are trying to accomplish. They make it happen. They can innovate on their own when it happens, if given the freedom. They recognize quickly the need for change and offer suggestions or adaptations.

Create an atmosphere or mind-set of *we* are in this together, and the "boss" is not the only person who has a creative brain in this whole outfit. Creating a "we" mind-set can only be done by continually asking for input. Don't merely ask for input—put the input into operation, so the "inputter" can see your value and appreciation for his or her contribution.

If asking for input is done on a continuing basis, and then nothing is done with the input, an attitude is soon communicated: "Why have input? It is never used or appreciated. I'm being conned." When this happens a negative attitude arises, and negation tends to slow matters down; the reverse of productivity occurs. Excuse this mundane illustration. It's like a farmer calling the hogs to the trough and never putting feed (or very little feed) into the trough. After a while, the hogs quit coming to the trough because what they receive isn't worth the effort to show up. It's more satisfying to "root" for oneself. It's a shame because, after all, the ultimate purpose of the hog is to give his life for the farmer's benefit.

The same is true of leaders if the continuation of "call to the trough" for input is not handled properly (the food in the trough being appreciation, recognition, awareness of acceptance, awards, and rewards—all types of factors that feed the individual's self-esteem). The result will be that positive input will cease. The attitude of the inputters will be, "I'll just 'root' around by myself. I'm not needed." A negative attitude of uselessness will develop, and the desired results will disappear. In reality, most people will give their lives to a cause that is worthy where their input is considered important.

When I was in a staff meeting, a person was continually feeding ideas to his supervisor of how operations and sales could be improved. They were good ideas. Finally, the irritated supervisor blurted out, "You are not paid to think. I'm paid to think, so quit thinking, and just do your job." This killed the incentive for the individual and the group.

What a tragedy when a leader thinks he or she is the

only person with a brain—or worse still, when leaders think they are the only ones to whom God speaks.

Therefore, lead for input. Put it into practice as soon as possible.

2. What Motivates People?

Many times people have the mistaken idea that leadership is a desire for power over people or situations. However, this is not totally true.

Many leaders are motivated by a clear idea of what they want. They have visions of what is needed and desired. In the scriptures, Proverbs 29:18 reads, "Where there is no vision, the people perish." How true this is. Unless you have a vision about where you want to go, what you want to accomplish, and how to arrive there, life can become a drag. Good leaders will set goals to accomplish the vision in mind. They will create in their goals the details in a step-by-step process toward achievement. Then they move a step at a time and in a sense transfer their dreams into reality. They can also have a realistic idea about when they will reach the goal.

Skilled leaders have a sense of urgency. Once they view the goal or have the vision, they will more clearly see and sense the eagerness to experience their stated goals. They will have the attitude of doing it now—no procrastination—and have a strong feeling of "must" for accomplishment. This puts the person ahead of the daydreamers or the thinkers who never activate their dreams.

Successful leaders have a strong sense of rightness. Once one has the clear vision and eagerness to see the images he has created in his mind, he will have a sense of fair play in regard to the quality of accomplishing the task. Sometimes, impatience may take over, and shortcuts may be attempted. In the long run, a skilled leader will be conscious of doing the job right, so he might be able to enjoy fulfillment when the vision has become reality.

Good leaders are capable of challenging others. They use communications skills to share their dream with other people in order to turn a dream into a realized accomplishment.

The visionary person readily accepts individual responsibility to accomplish the goal and seems to have a more intense passion for its accomplishment than those facilitators they may enlist around them. However, they soon learn to cope with any weakness in other people. The leader learns to accept this attitude, but at the same time realizes he/she must work as hard or harder than anyone else. He or she learns realistically the saying, "If it is to be, it is up to me."

Adept leaders, where they are lacking, learn to draw on the resources of others. Generally speaking, leaders have a better working knowledge of what they want to accomplish, but they do not have the resources to execute the plan to its fullest. This is why it is necessary for leaders to employ the expertise of others around them to accomplish the given task. Putting it all together gives the leader success. Therefore, intellect, experience, and a knowledge of people are real assets to excellent leadership.

In leadership, authority usually has plenty to do with accomplishments and contributions. However, in the final analysis we have to admit: those who get the most out of whatever is happening, whether or not such is selfishly motivated, are sometimes those who have given the most.

3. "Murphy's Law" Perversely Affects You

No one really seems to know where "Murphy's Law" originated, but here are some ideas from Murphy's Law:

- Nothing is as easy as it looks.
- Everything takes longer than you expect.
- If there is a possibility of several things going wrong, the one that goes wrong first will be the one that will do the most damage.
- Left to themselves, all things go from bad to worse.
- If you work on a thing only enough to improve it, it will break.
- If you think everything will be OK, you have surely overlooked something.
- Mother Nature always sides with the hidden flaw.

Your leadership can be affected by this attitude and invalidate some great ideas by not even attempting or trying to accomplish something for fear that Murphy's Law will take over. And yet, the antithesis of this statement is that many people seem to manage and live very happily through adversities. How do these people seem to accomplish this type of outlook on life? Let's search for some answers.

First, real happiness is a mind-set of the heart and not necessarily controlled by happenings. It seems strange that as one reads articles in newspapers of people who have everything financially in the world, and you would think would be very happy, but they commit suicide because of loneliness and being unhappy? Yet many times we read or hear of poverty-stricken families who have such tremendous joy and happiness, and yet have practically no mate-

rial possessions to speak of. So we discover happy people in
all kinds of circumstances among both rich and poor.

This does not mean we should not have visions and try to
move from one social level to another, but it does imply that
wherever we are, we should strive toward a healthy mental
attitude about being happy.

The apostle Paul stated, "I have learned, in whatsoever
state I am, therewith to be content" (Phil. 4:11). When Paul
wrote this he was in prison, and yet he gave us one of the
most positive outlooks on life in this and other epistles. We
can surely understand that happiness is not a function but
an attitude of the mind.

Second, coping with our situation depends on the outlook
we have on life. Recently, a friend's company had a reorga-
nization. Jobs were changed, and people were transferred
from one department to another. Approximately two
months passed, and no explanation was given about why
the change occurred or why people were transferred. Management made all the decisions but failed to communicate
to the personnel why the changes took place. Needless to
say, incentives, sense of accomplishment, direction, and
self-worth plummeted.

Finally, my friend was brave enough to ask upper management, "What was the purpose of the change? What are
you trying to accomplish? How do you see persons doing
their jobs to accomplish their goals?"

Upper management had assumed that middle management had carried out this function, but the latter had not.
Answers were given to all the questions asked, which
helped my friend at least begin to grasp the purpose of
some of the decisions. However, he is still waiting to see

what middle management does and if the information given him is accurate.

Leaders must understand that they have to convey to everyone involved the purpose of the change, the desired results, and where each person has a responsibility to help make it all work together.

One factor often left out is personal input by the individual who is supposed to accomplish the desired task. The individual needs a boost with a statement, an impression, or knowledge of certain factors.

Always keep in mind that when a person has sufficient input, he may well commit himself to a project. He may respond, "Here is the way I can accomplish my task." He may then buy into whatever is being decided and feel personally involved. This is one of the secrets of successful Japanese marketing and building of products. Each individual has an input into his part of the job to make the total venture a success.

4. Goal Setting

Goal setting is necessary each year if you're going to help a Sunday School class or department grow. Remember, the secret to success is involvement. The more people you have involved, the more successful your program is going to be.

Therefore, with this in mind, a Sunday School director or minister of education should not set the goal alone. The church may have a number in mind, but let the individuals in each class and department set their own enrollment goals. Then the Sunday School director can answer the question, "What is your enrollment goal for this next year or next quarter?"

Logan Carlisle, minister of education at Bethlehem Baptist Church in Clarksville, Georgia, picked up that concept, but he went a step further. He gave an 8½ x 11-inch sheet of paper to the class members and had them sign their names to the following statement:

> We believe that our Sunday School class can grow and reach new people for Christ this year. Our current class enrollment is _____ and our new class enrollment goal is _____.

Signature of Class Members

1. _____	9. _____
2. _____	10. _____
3. _____	11. _____
4. _____	12. _____
5. _____	13. _____
6. _____	14. _____
7. _____	15. _____
8. _____	

Please return with your records by next Sunday.

5. Types of Visitation/Contacts

A need in most of our churches is to broaden visitation. Consider changing the reference to visitation to the term *contacts*. The semantics of the word *visitation* conveys basically one methodology of reaching people, that is, door knocking.

When the word *contacts* is used, it opens the mind-set to a broader base of thinking in outreach to prospects and members of the Sunday School and church. The methodology when broadened conveys more than door knocking. It extends the thinking to telephoning, cards and letters, and casual contacts when an active member sees a prospect or absentee at a store, an office, or other places outside the home. This concept is called *constant contact consciousness* (24 hours a day, seven days a week). This becomes a lifestyle in outreach.

The use of the term *visitation* generally conveys a mind-set to a specific day of the week and a specific time of the day which is deemed necessary. However, with the above thinking in mind, encourage leadership to start using the term *contacts* interchangeably with the word *visitation,* thus broadening the base of outreach.

Several types of contacting are:

- prospect contacting;
- ministry to members;
- soul-winning visits;
- enrolling visit;
- prospect surveys;
- absentee contacts; and
- worker-enlistment contacts.

Prospect contacting . . . is when Sunday School class members or members of other organizations in the church (special studies, music, missions organizations, etc.) contact persons who are not members of Sunday School or their church organization. Generally, for the first contact with a prospect, personal contact at the home or on the job in a

face-to-face encounter by the class member is recom-
mended. This allows a more personal, intimate approach to
dialogue and questions to be asked and answered.

With the personal approach, two options can be given to
the prospect. The prospect can be given the invitation to be
a part of the class and to enroll in Sunday School. A new
member enrollment card can be filled out and returned to
the church office.

Ministry to members . . . is when a class is organized by
outreach groups or care groups (preferably one group leader
to every five persons enrolled). There is caring, praying, and
interest for one another. Ideally, a group leader keeps in
touch with all the members in that group by phone calls,
postcards, personal visits in the home, or casual contacts
outside the home. The group leader prays for group members and is alerted when a member is sick, has a death in
the family, goes to the hospital, and the like.

Soul-winning visitation . . . is being interested in the spiritual welfare of every member of the class. In a personal
one-to-one visit in the home, the office, or some other convenient place a group leader or other interested person contacts the unsaved person and makes an appointment to see
him to present the plan of salvation. The "Roman Road" is
widely used. It is simple and ideal for group leaders and
other interested people to use in soul-winning visitation.
There are many other approaches found in booklets and
tracts.

An enrolling visit . . . is when a contact is made with a
prospect in the home, office, or other place of meeting and
the prospect is encouraged to enroll in Sunday School and
become a part of a group studying God's Word. It is surpris-

ing that there are more people ready to be enrolled than most Sunday School workers realize. In my book *Beyond All Expectations,* there is a plan for high enrollment Sunday.

A prospect survey . . . is a method of finding prospects to increase Sunday School enrollment. Periodically, action should be taken to find prospects. This involves knocking on doors in the church community to find people who are not attending Sunday School. These people are prospects. Follow-up visits should be made to discover if the person is a bona fide prospect. In one sense of the word these "prospects" who are found in the prospect "hunt" are "suspects." A second or third contact may need to be made to enroll them and/or find out if they really are prospects. Once a quarter it is helpful to discover prospects in the morning worship service(s). More information in detail can be found in my *Motivational Ideas for Changing Lives* and *Beyond All Expectations.*

An absentee contact . . . is contacting absentees by cards, telephone calls, or casual visits in the grocery store, service station, etc. It is expressing to the absentee: "We missed you in Sunday School" or "We're looking for you in Sunday School this week." Allowing this broad sense of contacting involves more people. When contacts go up, attendance goes up. The reverse is also true. When contacts go down, so does the attendance. The scripture says, "As ye go, preach, . . . Heal . . . cleanse" (Matt. 10:7-8).

A worker-enlistment contact . . . is one of the major tasks of the Sunday School director, minister of education, and the nominating committee to keep the organization staffed with workers. Ideally, potential workers for the Sunday

School should be enlisted "eyeball-to-eyeball" through personal contact. The second way is by telephone, and a third is by letter. Other methods of worker enlistment can be done, but do not include or involve contact/visitation.

Another step in worker enlistment is enlisting the potential worker for training. This involves contacting as stated above and should be personal contacting. Sometimes for various reasons, another method might be used such as telephone, letters and cards, and seeing people in daily activities during the week. Other special methods of visitation/contacts can be made.

Do the following as a way to maximize your forces on visitation day/night by using the above concepts of visitation.

On visitation day/night in the fellowship hall (generally), tables are set up in the following manner:

- prospects only table;
- absentees (divided into four age-group tables);
- hospital, sick, Homebound, Cradle Roll table;
- cards and letter table (Stationery, cards, and pens should be available.);
- church members not enrolled in Sunday School table.

This gives members freedom of choice. Also, more involvement can take place. Other ideas of additional types of visitation/contact tables could be created. The beauty of this idea is: more people will become involved especially on visitation day/night because of the variety of methods and choices given to members of the Sunday School. Change this idea to fit your church and your people.

Remember, the secret to success is involvement. The more people you have involved, the more successful the program will be. What day/night should you have visitation? Set the time for when you can get the most people involved!

6. The Sunday School Evangelism Team

Successful evangelism in a church centers around cooperation of the Sunday School leadership—workers and teachers—plus an involvement of the church staff. Ideally, the pastor sets the tone for evangelism by encouraging the people to seek the unsaved for Bible study and preaching.

About 10 percent of a congregation could have the gift of soul-winning. In the average congregation, 20 percent can be committed for teaching and/or leadership responsibility.

An effective evangelism team can be built by class members, teachers, and pastor working together to reach people for Christ. The concept is simple:

1. The class members invite and bring lost acquaintances to Sunday School to hear the Word of God taught.

2. The teacher under the leadership of the Holy Spirit teaches the Word of God to prepare the lost persons for salvation.

3. The pastor through the preaching of the Word may gain a response for salvation and church membership.

Your church should provide training for those interested in winning persons for Christ.

"Who then is Paul, and who is Apollos, but ministers by whom ye believed, even as the Lord gave to every man? I have planted, Apollos watered; but God gave the increase. Now he that planteth and he that watereth are one: and every man shall receive his own reward according to his own labour. For we are labourers together with God: ye are God's husbandry, ye are God's building" (1 Cor. 3:5-9).

7. Inreach and Outreach for You: IOU

Purpose:

To involve Sunday School leadership and all members in an intense effort to *reach out* to prospects and "our own" members simultaneously. This provides a unified approach rather than concentrating on a particular group.

Theme:

"I.O.U.—I owe you . . . We do owe God plenty—our very lives—for what He did for us. This theme helps heighten *our* calling to the Great Commission and the awareness of our individual role in the process.

Methodology:

(1) Enlist support of Sunday School Council and church staff;

(2) Prepare list of class members for teachers and outreach leaders as well as a list of church members who are not enrolled in Sunday School;

(3) Have department leaders promote emphasis to teachers and explain specifics during the department period to all members;

(4) Pastor/minister of education/Sunday School director should discuss specifics with all teachers and enlist enthusiastic support;

(5) Set a date for high attendance and appropriate goals for Sunday School attendance and worship attendance;

(6) Develop posters and fliers for distribution. Fliers can be attached to class roll books;

(7) Provide a means of recording contacts weekly (3 x 5 cards or a special sheet; attach to a roll book with a paper clip);

(8) Promote, promote, promote! Talk it up with the minister of education or Sunday School director leading the

way by calling all general officers and department leaders each week;

(9) Determine the number of contacts made each week, number of those who make contacts, classes, and departments with good attendance, and the like. Publicize and promote the results weekly in bulletins, newsletters, and *from the pulpit;*

(10) On High Attendance Day publicize the number of contacts made during the emphasis, the number of contacters, and special happenings. Above all, highlight the efforts of teachers during the morning worship services by having department directors stand at the front and present a flower (rose, mum, apple or something like that) to each teacher as they come forward to their director. The pastor, minister of education, or Sunday School director should direct the procedures and express verbal appreciation to all who participated.

Benefits:

(1) It can increase Sunday School enrollment and attendance in proportion to the number of contacts made;

(2) It can be geared to fit a desired time frame (two to six weeks). The best is three to four weeks.

(3) It can involve teachers in the habit of contacting (visit, phone call, postcards). All members in the class are called.

(4) It involves care-group leaders and all members in the "reaching" process.

(5) It can help the adult class focus on class organization and sharpen relationship skills.

(6) It helps get the church in the mind-set of "constant contact consciousness" (CCC).

(7) It helps Sunday School members realize the ministry needs in their own class and understand the potential for reaching others;

(8) It provides a "reason" for having department social

times before Sunday School, either on high attendance or each Sunday during emphasis.

(9) It provides a greater understanding of what Sunday School should be and the responsibilities of each individual;

(10) It gives a format that lends itself to variation of methodology while yielding both tangible and intangible results.

(11) It helps some teachers to realize they have too many enrolled in their classes. This can ultimately lead to smaller classes and growth.

Charles Fox of Heritage Baptist Church in Annapolis, Maryland, created this idea. During that period of time there were 1,466 contacts; twenty new Sunday School members were added; one class had perfect attendance; there was an increase in enrollment from 694 to 714; and an attendance increase from 312 to 337. This was done during the month of March.

2
Prospect Ideas for Growth

8. Prospect 777:
How Long Do You Keep a Prospect?

I have often heard, "If a prospect file is over six months old, in all probability it is obsolete." This is likely true since there is a constant turnover of people in many communities. The fact is that one out of every five homes in America is built on wheels! This indicates that people are literally ready to move their total home, if necessary.

The question arises, "How long do we keep a prospect?" You will sometimes hear "until Jesus comes." This may be rather weak with no real direction, and it demotivates the desire for going after the same person month after month and year after year. So, there is a positive process one can follow in keeping up with the prospect.

Theoretically, you will start this idea in the month of October. Obviously, you may have new members who come in November, December, January, and so forth. So, keep the prospect in an active file for seven months. Keep in mind that prospects will be found during the other months of the year. But to catch this idea, let's think about your prospect file as a revolving file beginning in October. Each month as you add new prospects to the file, keep them for seven months. Seven months from October brings us into April, which generally is around Eastertime. Then have a High Enrollment Sunday. You can find more detailed information on how to do a high enrollment Sunday in my book *Beyond All Expectations.*

Assign each prospect to a Sunday School class and give that class the responsibility of reaching that person. Make a wall chart with all the prospects for that Sunday School class and place it in the class for high visibility. If we visualize what we want to happen, it more than likely will. On the chart put the following columns: a column listing the prospect names, one with the total home visits, one for the phone calls, and another for the postcards.

During the seven-month period, make sure to keep up with a prospect. See that seven postcards are sent to the person during the seven-month period. It is best to have a class member choose a prospect to contact. During the second week have the same person make a phone contact with the person he or she wrote a card to the first week. During the third week encourage class members to go by and make a face-to-face contact. Follow the same plan for each prospect. Use the postcard first, which lowers the anxiety of most class members when making contact with a prospect. During the phone call one can always refer back to, "Did you get my card last week? I'm the person who sent it. We'd like to have you in our Sunday School class." A simple type of conversation as suggested can be used.

By the third week, the prospect is familiar with the class member because of the postcard or the phone call, and an appointment could be made during the call. ("Could I come by your house and visit you next week?") After these three initial contacts are made to the prospect during the first cycle, then any class member who wants to send a postcard, make a phone call, or go by and visit can do so. The idea, of course, is that during a seven-month period seven post-cards, seven phone calls, and seven home visits are made. This gives a class a variety and time frame in which to work.

In all probability the prospects, during this period of time, may have come to the class and/or joined, or it will be discovered they really never were prospects at all. At the end of the seven-month period, there should have been at least twenty-one contacts. In all probability, with this many contacts being made to one individual, he or she will join the Sunday School before all the contacts are completed—or either ask that you stop contacting them.

However, in the event the persons do not join the Sunday School class in the seven-month period, remove their names and put them into a holding file for five months. When a twelve-month period has passed—that is, the seven months of concentrated contacting and five months of no contact at all—the fact of no contact being made may have an effect. The high level of contact the previous seven months may many times cause a person to make a decision.

At the end of the twelve-month period, prospects are assigned to a new class, and the same process is repeated. The new class sends the seven postcards, makes seven phone calls, and makes seven home visits.

9. Husband and Wife Reaching Young Marrieds

Create a new unit by teaming up a husband and wife to reach newlyweds and young marrieds. The husband and wife should model quality mate interaction, share outreach efforts, and lead in Bible teaching and fellowship.

Young adults are assimilated more quickly than when only one person is the class leader. Newlyweds especially have responded well to this approach in class growth. Both males and females will have a role model in the class. Neither mate is made to feel awkward.

Bo Prosser of First Baptist Church in Roswell, Georgia, is using this idea and already has created three young married classes as new units. Each class begins with a list of names on paper. Within six months each class has had at least twenty on roll and ten to twelve in attendance. Care has been given to build a strong base of fellowship as well as Bible teaching. The two are necessary.

After the class has stabilized, usually within a period of six to nine months, a permanent teacher is selected for the class, and the move is made for the teaching couple to start another unit. At this writing, all three classes are doing well, all are still growing, all are strong, and the fellowship with these young couples is exciting.

People go where they know they are wanted. The Lord is blessing the efforts. The last time I checked the church had grown from 550 to 800 average attendance in Sunday School.

The secret is contacting does the job.

10. A Chicken Way to Prospect

The church makes arrangement with a chicken fast food service in the community as a welcome to new families who move into the community and as a public relations gesture to give a box or bucket of chicken to newcomers.

You may even want to make arrangements with a local soft drink/bottling company or a grocery store to do the same. The idea is that the church finds a prospective new family that has moved to town. As soon as the church is aware or even while the prospect is in the process of moving in, the church calls one of their senior adults who is on a list and has already volunteered to deliver the chicken and cold drinks in a cooler to the new family.

The church not only contacts the senior adult but also the chicken and the cold drink places that one of their senior adults will be by to pick up the food and drinks. The chicken and cold drink place inserts a card or flyer or some identification as a welcome to the neighborhood, and the church also inserts its identification. When the chicken is delivered, the person doing the delivering greets the new-comers and invites them to church. "We at the Church along with these friends of yours say welcome."

11. Prospect Cards in the Class/Department

Use cards to list prospects with their phone numbers and addresses. Mount the cards on a wall underneath a large sign that reads *prospects.*

Every class should be able to see its prospects and be constantly reminded about outreach. The key encouraging people to select the prospects is in the corner of each card identifying the type of prospect it is. Place initials in the right-hand lower corner, such as *CM.* This indicates a church member not enrolled in Sunday School. A *P* indicates a parent of a child. *BE* indicates a Baptist elsewhere (someone who has moved to town and their church membership is elsewhere). An *L* indicates lost. *U* indicates unknown.

At the close of the class period, the teacher can encourage the pupils to turn to next Sunday's lesson, calling it by the title of the lesson and urging the pupils to study during the week. At the same time, the teacher should encourage them to look on the wall and write down the name of a prospect. People will often choose certain prospects because their awareness about the type of prospect can lower the fear level. For example, if one knows a person is a church member not enrolled in Sunday School, he/she is more likely to accept the name of the person and make contact by a phone call or a postcard. Many people do not have anxiety in contacting a Baptist elsewhere or a parent of a child because of identification. On visitation night, the unknown prospects or lost prospects should be concentrated on, especially if a church has a group of people who have been through special witnessing training or evangelistic programs.

12. Instant Cradle Roll/Homebound Prospects

In the main auditorium, distribute 3 x 5 cards to the entire congregation. This idea can be carried out on Sunday morning, Sunday evening, or Wednesday night. Announce to the congregation, "Do you know someone who doesn't attend? Who has children two years and younger, or who is expecting a child?" Have them write the name, address, and phone number of those persons. At the top of the card write *Cradle Roll Prospect*. Then on the flip side of the same card, write the word *Homebound* at the top. The question is asked, "Do you know anyone who does not attend and is a shut-in, an invalid, and/or Homebound?" It is advisable to expand on the word *homebound* because many people do not understand or know what the term means. One you might describe as homebound may not necessarily be an older person. In all probability, however, most of them will be older people. Write their names, addresses, and phone numbers on the card. If your church or Sunday School does not have a Homebound or Cradle Roll Department, this would be an excellent way to start. Every congregation has these two types of prospects because babies are always being born and people are getting older. Until those two functions of life cease, every Sunday School in the entire country should have a Cradle Roll and Homebound ministry.

13. Pin-Back Buttons

This idea uses pin-back buttons as a conversation opener. Print the following letters on a brightly colored pin-back button: *AYGTBISS*. These letters on the pin mean, "Are you going to be in Sunday School?"

Most people are curious. Inquiries will probably be made about the pin, and people wearing the pin will be able to answer the question, inviting the person to Sunday School at the same time.

This idea was implemented by First Baptist Church of Newalla, Oklahoma. Russ Houser is the minister of education. The congregation employed the idea for four weeks during the fall period preparing for their Sunday School reunion. The cost of the pins was inexpensive, and people wore them for a number of weeks after the campaign emphasis.

14. Prospecting with Service in Mind

Don Allen of Southwood Baptist Church, Oklahoma City, gave this idea called *Senior Seekers.* Senior Seekers form a group made up of adults who are age fifty-five and older and still mobile. This group targets rest homes and retirement centers for the elderly. Mailouts are sent to each of the people on the list in these homes. They are given the opportunity to attend a program once a month held within the building between the hours of 11 AM until noon. The program consists of thirty minutes of singing and thirty minutes of Bible teaching and preaching. At twelve o'clock a special meal is brought in by the church. This is worked out with the retirement center, so there is no conflict. Then there is time for prayer requests and recognition of birthdays, anniversaries, and other important dates for the folks.

These people are given the opportunity to become members of the Homebound ministry or a senior adult class; they have the opportunity to attend the church if they are able. They are asked to name prospects for the church, such as their children, grandchildren, relatives, and friends who live in the community and do not attend another church.

Many churches are endeavoring to reach people in retirement centers and rest homes, providing ministries through the weekdays and on Sunday morning. Some church members are going by the church office on Sunday morning, picking up the record box, riding a van, going to the retirement center, and teaching Sunday School.

The Sunday School record is turned in, and the senior adults have the opportunity to attend the worship services. After services they return via the van to the retirement center.

There are some advantages to this approach. There is no church space, heat, lights, or furniture required for classrooms. The only expense is for additional literature and transportation in going to pick up these people.

15. Senior Day at High School

Pastoring and operating a Sunday School in a mountain mission area is not always easy. *Pastor Ronald Kinzel, Sr., in Eastern Kentucky ran into a problem on graduation when the school decided not to have a baccalaureate service.* Many of the students were upset as this was a traditional activity. Therefore, the pastor decided he would have the baccalaureate service on Sunday in the church since eight of the high school seniors were active in the church program. Contact was made with the high school principal. The idea presented was accepted with a great deal of pleasure. Arrangements were made for meetings with the senior faculty, sponsors, and students. Invitations were given to friends by letter and personal invitation at the school. Parents were invited by a personal letter from the pastor.

A reception from 2:00 to 3:00 PM with students, teachers, parents, and church members was held. All of this was videotaped for a future time capsule on the tenth anniversary of the graduating class. From 3:00 PM until 4:00 PM, tribute was given to the parents, the teachers, and the students. The principal spoke, and the school chorus brought special music. Seniors from the church had special music. A slide presentation of the number of activities that had taken place during the past four years was given. A special message was brought by a Christian layman who was a former graduate of the high school and who now was a successful local attorney. The eight graduating seniors from the church were instructed ahead of time to bring something they wanted to save for their tenth class reunion and to place it in a time capsule to be opened at a future date. Every graduating senior was given a *Good News Bible,* was personally interviewed on videotape, and asked questions about plans for the future.

An additional benefit was that the local cable television station played the videotapes three times at later dates by requests of local merchants and people in the area. From this activity a prospect list was made from the names and addresses of students, parents, and friends not attending this church. There were eighty-five graduates, all were present including out-of-town relatives. New church members were gained as a result of this activity. Prospects are still being contacted. The church received high visibility in the community, and all of it was free because they recognized senior day as an outreach opportunity.

16. "Forty-Niners" Club

In this idea the congregation is encouraged to locate prospects. Each person who is a prospect is considered a gold nugget. Once persons have discovered ten gold nuggets, they are a member of the "Forty-Niners" Club. They are recognized in a morning worship service with a certificate and pin to wear identifying them as "Forty-Niners." The pin serves as recognition for the person and advertisement for the promotion. The goal is to have forty-nine people find ten prospects or more and become members of the "Forty-Niners" Club. The first several people to be recognized as "Forty-Niners" surprisingly were senior adults, said *Glenn Thompson, Sunday School director of the Sharon Baptist Church in Wichita, Kansas*. They went beyond their goal of forty-nine people. When one looks at the idea it seems as if they were trying to get 490 prospects, but actually it went beyond the 700 mark. Many people found two, three, and four prospects but never reached their goal of ten prospects to get their forty-nine pin.

Glenn said this idea should be tried at least once a year to boost the prospect file with fresh prospects and enthusiasm in the congregation.

17. One Free Dinner

Dr. Ronald Skaggs, minister of education, First Baptist Church, Muskogee, Oklahoma, has a unique way of using a 4 x 6-inch card. One side of the card says, "This card good for one free dinner and lots of new friends." The first paragraph reads, "Here is some food for thought. Are you interested in being part of a new family? A family dedicated to worshiping God together and helping each other along life's journey? At First Baptist Church, you will meet people just like yourself, working and worshiping together. Enjoy Wednesday night meals and fellowship. Please pray about whether this is where your family belongs. (Dinner is served at 6:15 PM.)" Then at the bottom of the card it says, "Please fill out the information on the back so we may know you better." On the reverse side of the card there is a place to write the family name, address, and telephone number. There are seven spaces under the family name for the given name of the person, the relationship, the birthdate, school grade, and Christian (yes or no). The relationship is used with initials *H* for husband, *W* for wife, *D* for daughter, and *S* for son.

Ronald indicated this has been one of their most effective ways of reaching people. These cards are given out to all prospects by the members both in visitation with families, business associates, and people they meet in other activities throughout the city.

The members carry a number of these cards and freely distribute them. They are picked up from the visitors when they come to the Wednesday night fellowship dinner. The cards are used as a ticket for the family when they attend the supper.

18. CARE: *Contact and Reach Everyone*

This is a Sunday School-wide program lasting fourteen weeks. Generally, it is ideal to conduct from January through the first Sunday in April.

A CARE program is designed to put classes into friendly competition with one another as emphases are made on contacting and reaching prospects for Sunday School. It is an outreach and inreach program for the church. Each week, points for making contacts and reaching prospects are awarded to each class. At the end of the fourteen weeks, make an award of some type, like a plaque, to each age group division (preschool, children, youth, and adults), and then one plaque for the class with the highest overall total points for the entire period.

Points are obtained by doing the following activities and reporting them in the Sunday School records.

> 100 points for: contacting 100 percent of members. (These can be visits, cards, and phone calls.)
>
> 50 points for: contacting at least 75 percent of absent members.
>
> 5 points for: each prospect visit made. (This must be a personal, face-to-face contact made that includes an invitation or encouragement to attend Sunday School.) Note: When you visit in the home of a prospect and there are four members of the family there, you count the number of prospect visits made as four. When you

invite a fellow worker or classmate to attend Sunday
School, it is counted as one prospect visit made.

10 points for: each other prospect contact made. (This is
for the contacts to prospects made by phone, cards, letters, and so forth).
Note: Ten points are counted for each phone call, card,
or letter, no matter how many members there are in
the family of the prospect.

50 points for: each visitor present in your class. (A visitor's slip must be turned in in order for the visitor to be
counted. A visitor is one who is not a member of any
class or department in the Sunday School.)

150 points for: each new member enrolled in class. (A new
member slip must be turned in for the new member to
be counted. A new member is a person who is not cur-
rently a member of a class or department in the Sunday School.)

Points can be awarded only for efforts in contacting and
reaching to be reported on a regular, weekly Sunday School
record. Each class must fill in all of the appropriate information on the records each week. Points are based on the
information sent in by the classes.

During those fourteen weeks, the class has an enjoyable
experience showing that class members do CARE! Now the
acrostic of CARE means *Contact and Reach Everyone.*

*Joe Borgkbist gave us this idea from First Baptist
Church, West Columbia, South Carolina. Joe is minister of
education.* He suggested a good time to work on this idea
may be during the summertime, since it will offset the
"summer slump." He has used the idea both in the summer
and the first quarter of the year.

In the summer, the increase was 12 percent. In the first
quarter, it was 11 percent. He suggested that the plaques

awarded stay in the class or department for an entire year. When the program is repeated a year or so later, the plaques circulate with a new class name etched on the plate. The results for this church during the first quarter of the year were:

- Average weekly attendance increased 11 percent from 247 to 274.
- High attendance was 322 compared to 285 the previous year.
- Low attendance was 255, compared to 219 the previous year.
- There were 200 visitors in Sunday School, compared to 158 the previous year.
- There were 42 new members enrolled, compared to six the previous year.
- Offerings increased 13 percent from $63,791 to $72,090.
- The spirit of outreach enthusiasm was higher among younger-age classes than the older ones.

Joe suggested that you implement the idea for a full quarter. This allows those involved to see marked increases and results instead of just working for several weeks or a month at a time. It also emphasizes when the contacts go up, the attendance increases, new members join, and other aspects advance.

Another added benefit is that a certificate was awarded to each class/department that reported 100-percent absentee contacts at least ten of the fourteen weeks. This included nine of the eleven classes who were age fifty and up. A permanent plaque was awarded to the runner-up adult division because of the large number of adult classes.

The final results were over 5,500 contacts, with over 4,100 absentee contacts. There were 964 prospect visits reported. A record number of visitors attended (over 200) and 42 out of 200 enrolled in Sunday School. The ongoing benefits for the next quarter were: contacts remained higher than before, as did average attendance.

19. Intercessory Prayer for Prospects

Fielder Road Baptist Church in Arlington, Texas, has a unique way of reaching people and praying for them (intercessory prayer) for all guests who attend the worship services. During the worship service, a visitor's slip is handed out with basic information of name, address, city, zip, birthday, and phone.

The information is divided into four groups such as preschool, student grades, single adults, and married adults in categories of twenties, thirties, forties, fifties, and sixties.

Additional information is requested, such as member of what church and where? (with four questions for the guest to check in the box) guest for the first time? new in the community? would you like to unite with the church? or would you like a staff visit? The guest is asked to fill this out and place the slip in the offering plate.

This piece of information is distributed to people during prayer meeting, asking them to pray for this guest. The following information is given on a separate slip of paper, along with the slip the visitor filled out. To the person who is going to pray, the slip states, "Intercessory Prayer for Worship Service Guests."

Then it says:

Note to Intercessors: The person(s) whose names you see on this card were our worship guests on Sunday. Please pray for them and give them a call at home, preferably in early evening (since most people work during the day). If you cannot reach them, please mail them a prayergram.

If you do contact them, say, "Hello, I'm (name) from _____ Church. I'm part of our intercessory prayer ministry. You were our guest Sunday, and we were pleased you came. I prayed for you today, so I wanted to call and ask if you have a special need you would appreciate our praying about this week. Perhaps you have a need in your family or elsewhere. Would you like us to remember you today?" (Let them respond.) Close the conversation by thanking them.

Remember the only purpose in calling is intercessory prayer; not to invite them to church. Pray for them without any conditions, favors, or expectations from them. This gives real meaning and integrity to your call. Discard this sheet and card when you have prayed.

The church also provides paper with space to write a note to the guest. On the reverse side after the sheet is folded, in bold letters the sheet says, "Prayergram, _____ Church." Then a Scripture verse is quoted at the bottom. "They that wait upon the Lord shall renew their strength" (Isa. 40:31). Also on the reverse side is information about the intercessory prayer chapel (if there is one) with the phone number and church address. Along with the prayergram is an envelope in which to mail it. The church picks up these notes, provides the stamps, and mails them through the church office.

Personal comment by author: This is a low-key soft sell about the church's high interest in the individual. Most church people really do care, and they are interested in people without high pressure to join other activities of the church. This places the church on a spiritual level and moves away from the traditional number consciousness that many churches display. *Thanks, Don Hull.*

20. Prospect Cemetery

A small town in central Texas is called Prospect. Near the highway is a sign that points up a country road to the town cemetery. I thought the words on the sign were amusing: "Prospect Cemetery." It has crossed my mind a number of times: How many churches, in a sense, have a prospect cemetery? That is, they find the prospects, put them in a file box, and place the box on a bottom shelf in a closet somewhere.

In a sense, all of these prospects went to the cemetery. How sad! When we do not make contacts with our prospects, we are relegating those people to a *Christless* grave. May your church never have a prospect cemetery!

21. How's Your Pulse?

This idea is geared primarily to senior adults 55 and older. *At Sam Hendry's church, First Baptist Church in Ardmore, Oklahoma,* emphases each month (usually the third Thursday at noon) include a time of food, fun, fellowship, and frivolity. Each senior adult is encouraged to bring a covered dish and a friend. This reaches the community, not only the senior adult church members.

It is primarily designed for fellowship and for senior adults who attend no church. Each month, emphasis is placed on helping the senior adults. Each quarter, several volunteer nurses are available to take their blood pressure and pulse, record other vital signs, and keep a record of them. The nurses give suggestions about how the senior adults may take better care of themselves. Humorous skits are provided during the fellowship time. Each month features a basic theme derived generally from a major activity or holiday.

22. Ministry in Motion

Pastor Gary Johnson from First Baptist, Winthrop Harbor, Illinois, has eight ministry teams. Each team leader is a deacon. The teams are as follow:

(1) *Welcome Wagon*—new home ministry, business participation, and welcome packet content. The leader's responsibility is to contact, distribute, and minister through newcomer information.

(2) *Helps and needs*—counseling and listening. This involves helping a person through a hard time such as divorce or death.

(3) *New members and Discipleship*—New member orientation or other discipling information. This team helps a new member get started.

(4) *Soul-winning*—Sharing the gospel. This group concentrates on personal-testimony witnessing.

(5) *Fellowship and support*—This team provides a "caring" ministry by integrating the church into the home and reclaiming unfaithful members.

(6) *Prospects*—This team contacts the weekly visitors, distributes prospects to other groups, and develops initial church contact.

(7) *Prayer group*—This team meets weekly for prayer, personally supports other teams and also the ministry taking place in the total church program.

(8) *Senior adults*—Shut-in ministry. This team plans and coordinates senior adult activities and ministers to senior adults.

A deacon or Sunday School teacher is in charge of the ministry teams. That person coordinates the ministry action for his group during deacons or Sunday School workers meetings. The person relates the activities of the ministry to the rest of the team.

Ministry in action could take place on Tuesday morning at 10:30 to noon, Wednesday evening at 7:15 to 8:15 PM, Thursday evening 6:30 to 8:00 PM, or any other time coordinated by the team leader.

23. Best Prospects

Pastor Kenneth Kyker, Antioch Baptist Church, Johnson City, Tennessee, discovered 785 names by using the following methodology of talking to people. Each class member was given a form sheet that had eighteen different types of people the class members come in contact with. Members were asked to jot down names, addresses and phone numbers, if possible, of different people of which they were aware. Out of the 785 names listed they found eighty-nine best prospects. There were sixty-five people in dire need, and ninety-five people who needed Christ as Savior. Many other prospects were listed beyond the one type as found in number 16.

Below is the form he used:

Name of Sunday School Member _____
Address _____
Phone Number _____
Name of Sunday School Teacher _____

How to interpret the following questions. Some names may be listed several times in this questionnaire.

    1. Best friend _____
       Other friends _____

_____

2. Closest relative (lives closest to you) not in your house

_____

3. Your supervisor at work (if none, write none)

_____

4. Person you supervise at work (or none) _____
5. A fellow worker _____
6. Friend at school _____
7. Person you ride to work with or have lunch with at work

_____

8. A single adult _____
9. Person you would call next week to go somewhere (shopping, ball game, hunting, fishing, so forth) ___
10. Person who recently had a baby _____
11. Person who recently moved into your neighborhood

_____

12. Person who recently got a promotion at work _____

_____

13. Person who recently lost a loved one (death in the family)

_____

14. Person who was recently divorced _____
15. A student at a nearby college _____
16. The best prospect for our church _____
17. Person in need (list the need) _____
18. Person who needs Christ as Savior _____

Please use the following code below behind each person's name to indicate what age groups he/she is in:

Adult = A
Young Adult = YD
Youth = Y

Children = C
Preschool = P

This idea should be used at least once a year during a Sunday School class hour.

24. Thursday Callers

Churches which have Wednesday night dinners can effectively use this idea. As a centerpiece on each table use a 3 x 5 card folded in half with a slit in the top of the fold. The slit holds other photo copies of visitors from Sunday services, plus a sheet of instructions. The people sitting at the table are asked to take one of the slips and on Thursday to give the visitor a phone call, telling him/her how good it was to have them visit the church on the past Sunday.

Don Hull, Fielder Road Baptist Church, Arlington, Texas, used this idea with a total of forty-eight tables with eight people seated around each table. The idea was to make 48 contacts each week. He used an alternative method of contact each week such as "Thursday Card Writers." This gave variety and variation to the program since some people may feel more at ease sending a postcard compared to making the phone call. The idea is excellent for making contacts with new people. This is in addition to the Monday night visitation when contact is made by visiting each prospect at home. Don reported that people are impressed by the contacts of the church members. A sample of the telephone conversation could be as:

> You were our guest Sunday and we were pleased you came. I prayed for you today, so I wanted to call and ask if you have a special need you would appreciate our praying about this week. Perhaps you have a need in your family?

Would you like us to remember you today?" (Let them respond.) Close the conversation by thanking them.

Remember our only purpose in calling is intercessory prayer; not to invite them to church. Do not turn the conversation away from prayer. Pray for them without any conditions, favors, or expectations from them. This gives real meaning and integrity to your call. Discard this sheet and card when you have prayed.

The church also provides paper with space to write a note to the guest. On the reverse side, after the sheet is folded, in bold letters at the top of the fold is: the Prayergram, Fielder Road Baptist Church, with a Scripture verse is quoted at the bottom. "They that wait upon the Lord shall renew their strength" (Isa. 40:31). Also on the reverse side is information about the intercessory prayer chapel with the phone number and church address for instance:

25. Christian Computer Camp

Computers are becoming a necessity much like automobiles were fifty and sixty years ago. Today most every American home feels the importance of having at least one automobile. In a short time, the same attitude about the computer/word processor will prevail.

With this in mind, *Dr. Charles Stone, pastor of Greater Gwinnett Baptist Church in Duluth, Georgia,* has a computer camp every year. The camp is for middle-school children whose parents want their children to gain a head start on the use of computers in this high-tech age. The camp is limited to twenty-five children. The fee is $25 per child (which covers all computer time, supplies, and refreshments.) The school begins on a Sunday evening and ends the following Friday. Parents' night is Friday from 6:30-8:00.

The following description gives parents an idea of what the camp is for:

Using a team approach, your child will learn to: (1) discover the parts of a computer system and what each part does; (2) use the computer in an innovative way to discover principles for successful living found in the Bible (that is, improving family relationships, choosing friends, and developing a positive attitude); (3) develop a simple interactive program on the computer that uses a speech synthesizer and a graphic board.

Offering this opportunity to children both inside and outside the church provides a good flow of prospective families for the church. Several families have been reached because of this innovative approach.

26. Prospect Auction

On Wednesday night or Sunday night, prospect packet cards and envelopes with prospect information are "bid off" to the people in the congregation. Seven days a week many of the congregation do their contacting during business hours, lunch hours, and evenings at home. Many times it becomes difficult for people to show up at the church on visitation evening, but it is helpful if the members can make the contacts all during the week. They turn in their packets the following Sunday in Sunday School. More people are visiting because of the motivation created by others accepting assignments.

A positive atmosphere is created by reports from last week's assignments in the form of a testimony meeting.

On Monday and Tuesday before the Wednesday night services, the church staff and/or outreach officers take surveys of visits to newcomers, visitors from the previous Sunday, and referrals.

Bob Fuston, associate state Sunday School director, Baptist General Convention of Texas, said, "In larger cities where people live a good distance from the church, Prospect Auction helps people stay involved in the outreach program."

27. SOS: Search Out Souls

SOS stands for "Search Out Souls." The idea is to find prospects for Sunday School by: leading each class and/or department, depending on the size of the church, to select either a Saturday or Sunday, and go out to certain sections of the town, knocking on doors looking for prospects.

This allows several things to happen:

(1) The church has an ongoing outreach program.

(2) Through summer months when an aggressive visitation program often slumps, SOS changes the trend.

(3) Each class and/or department works on a project and chooses which Saturday or Sunday it wants to visit door-to-door. Each class can have anywhere from two people to as many people as volunteer, seeking prospect information about people who live in the church area. The entire Sunday School does not assume the people search on one weekend but spreads it over the whole thirteen-week period.

The advantage is that all of the information does not pour in at one time. Many times churches will do this type of emphasis several times a year.

28. NARF:
Neighbor/Associate/Relative/Friend

The NARF Card idea can be used during a four-week promotional system. The first phase is to advertise the project by telling the congregation it needs to make a stab at what they think a Narf is and write their ideas on a card with their name and address. The person with the correct guess will receive a meal for two at Wednesday night supper.

To build excitement from the pulpit, share some of the ideas. Do this for the next two weeks. At the end of the AM service on the third week, explain that NARF stands for neighbor, associate, relative, or friend. Explain that the person who brings the most NARFs on NARF Sunday will win a dinner for two at a local restaurant. This can work not only for high attendance Sundays but also can gain prospects.

Thank you, Gary Stanton, Midwestern Baptist Theological Seminary, Kansas City, Missouri, for this idea.

3
Inreach Ideas
for Growth

29. New Member 333

Many churches are emphasizing that when one joins the church, he is joining the *whole* church. This idea came from my book *Motivational Ideas for Changing Lives*. I have promoted this idea for over twenty-five years. The idea is that when persons come down the aisle joining the church and are not members of the Sunday School, they automatically are enrolled. The weakness in this idea of joining the *whole* church is that sometimes Sunday School classes are not aware new members have been placed on their rolls. Thus, no effort is made to involve the new member and incorporate him into the activity of the Sunday School class. Therefore, the following process will help accomplish the task of leading the new member to become involved.

Make a poster with the new members' names on it in column form. The poster can be placed in a Sunday School classroom for high visibility and to remind the class members that new members have been enrolled. Keep the people's names on the list three months or until they attend. Send three postcards and make three phone calls and three home visits during the next three months. All new members should be contacted at least nine times. When the new members become active, their names are then deleted from the poster.

30. Enter and Sit Down, Please!

The Roswell First Baptist Church, Georgia, has a unique way of finding prospects. They ask in all of their worship services for people to fill out a registration card. This is given to the individual as they enter into the worship auditorium. This allows the staff to keep up not only with the membership but to quickly find visitors or prospects for the Sunday School and other organizations of the church.

This is especially effective in the eleven o'clock worship hour as guests are handed their bulletins, and the registration cards are enclosed when they arrive for the worship service. During the welcome part of worship, the pastor calls attention to the card and asks for everyone in the congregation to fill it out and pass it to the end of the pew. During the offertory hymn, the ushers collect all the cards.

On Sunday afternoon the pastor goes through the cards which have already been sorted into members and guests. On Monday morning, the outreach secretary makes a pocket-and-file prospect card for the prospect file. Each Monday afternoon at staff meeting, a staff member is assigned eight to ten prospects to contact during the week. The pastor challenges each staff member that every contact made he will match. *Thanks, Bo Prosser*

31. Spring March to Victory

Rev. Bill Tharp, First Baptist Church, Pearland, TX, 77581, gives this growth experience. For nine months the church was pastorless. When it looked as if the new pastor were coming, this campaign created four weeks in advance was called "Spring March to Victory in Sunday School." The whole idea was given over to reaching people for a high attendance when the pastor arrived. The Sundays were called *Battle One, Battle Two, Battle Three,* and *Battle Four.* The Saturday before Sunday *Battle One* was directed toward "inactive and absentee members." On that Sunday the emphasis was "Save Me a Seat in Sunday School." Everyone enrolled in Sunday School had his name on the back of a chair in the classes and departments, and everyone in attendance was given a medal for winning the battle on that Sunday.

Battle Two ("Mountain of Unenrolled Friends").

On the Saturday prior to *Battle Two,* the plan was for outreach. The afternoon visitation was given over to marching towards "friends and prospects" to be present in Sunday School.

Battle Three ("Prospect Hill").

The Saturday before the emphasis was for outreach, "marching to prospects," and literature distribution. The emphasis on Sunday was "Grandparents' Day" in the Sunday School.

Battle Four ("City of Faithfulville").

On the Saturday before the "Fall in for Outreach" was toward faithful members present on Sunday. On Sunday the emphasis was "Call the Roll Celebration Sunday." Each department and class would call the roll of all the troops in their Sunday School to see who was present.

The campaign revolved around major thoughts and actions, according to Tharp.

1. We are in God's people-reaching army.
2. We are clothed in His battle armor.

3. We "outreach" for four straight Sundays and spotlight four groups/actions. That is, (1) save me a seat, (2) friends, (3) grandparents, and (4) call the roll day.
4. We called each Saturday visitation a "battle" and named it for the group of people we aimed for.

The results of the campaign:

1. More people participated during Saturday visitation than regular Monday-night visitation. The highest number of outreachers was seventy-five.
2. For four consecutive Sundays attendance was over 800. That had not happened in over ten years. It's difficult to argue against success.

32. MIAs of the Sunday School

Nationwide there is a high level of interest in MIAs (service personnel *missing in action*). We do not know if these people are alive or dead or even where they are. So it is in many Sunday Schools across the nation.

There are people on Sunday School rolls who have not been seen, heard, or counted present in twelve or more months. These people are *MIAs—missing in attendance.*

The Sunday School many times does not know if these people are alive or dead. We can almost assume they are struggling spiritually because the Word of God says, "Forsake not the assembling of yourselves together" and "grow in grace and in the knowledge of our Lord and Savior Jesus Christ."

A way to call attention and lead the regular attending members to be concerned about their class of *MIAs* and to make contact is to give high visibility to these people.

You have probably seen or are aware of the contact idea: ABSENT   PRESENT   PROSPECTS. List all class members on a 3 x 5 card in column form mounted on the wall. At the beginning of the class, the teacher, outreach leader, or secretary places all member cards under the absent column. When a person comes into the room, their card is moved from the absent to the present column. At the close of the class, the teacher might say, "Look at the absent column and see who is absent. Pick out two names and turn to next Sunday's lesson. Write the two absentees' names and phone numbers on the first page of next Sunday's lesson. When you study Sunday's lesson, give the absentees a call, and tell them you missed them. Also pick out one prospect's name, write that name and phone number on the same Sunday School lesson. Give them a call." (For more information on this idea, look in the book *Beyond All Expectations,* pages 101-104.)

To make class members aware, become involved, and minister to the *MIAs,* add another column to the absent/ present/prospect so it appears as follows:

ABSENT   PRESENT   PROSPECT   MIAs

At the close of the class period, the teacher will suggest, "Look at the wall of absentees. Pick out two absentees, one prospect, and one *MIA.* Write the names and phone numbers at the top of the page in your quarterly. This week when you study your lesson, give them a phone call, or if you see the person on the street, at the store, or wherever, tell them you missed them in Sunday School."

Remember, you do not remove a name from the roll unless the person moves, joins another church, or dies. You transfer the person's name to a *"MIA"* roll if there has been no attendance for twelve months or more. In a sense, you create a high-priority prospect list.

The secret of success is involvement. The more people you have involved in contacting, the better your attendance will be.

Let us pray for and search out diligently for the *MIAs* on our Sunday School rolls.

Special Note: Class motivation to enroll more members drops considerably when a class's attendance drops below 40 percent. A "norm" is for attendance to run 40 to 60 percent. From time to time, you will have a bad Sunday or two, generally because of winter or holidays. We are thinking, basically, on a quarter-to-quarter basis.

When you run 30 percent, you need to examine why this is happening. (For more information, see *Motivational Ideas for Changing Lives,* pages 79-82.) When the attendance runs 20 percent, you are in real trouble and need to update the Sunday School roll. (For more information, see *Beyond All Expectations,* pages 86-90.)

33. Don't Be an Absent—Tee

Mail a card to each member in Sunday School. The card should have two holes punched on the right-hand side of the card, beginning about one inch from the top of the card. Place a golf tee into the two holes. The card should have printed on it in big, bold letters, "Don't be an absent—tee. Be "teed" off for the upcoming "drive." There is a "fair way." Don't be a "putter" but be a part of the "foursome."

Adapt the card or change it to fit your own situation and emphasis. It is suggested that you match up three Sunday School class members and one prospect to make up a foursome for High Attendance Day. This will give you opportunities for high attendance and new members in Sunday School. "Don't be an absent—tee" could be printed on the golf tee for this idea. *Louis Bratton, Jr., from Highland Baptist Church, Florence, Alabama,* submitted this idea.

34. Sunday School at Night

Create a new teaching unit on Sunday evening for Sunday School workers. These workers (preschool, children, and youth workers) do not have the opportunity of meeting with a group of adults because they are working elsewhere in Sunday School. However, many want adult Bible study.

Sunday School director Walter Rarrick, First Baptist Church, Springfield, Missouri, shared this idea, who says he enjoys going to the class because it gives him Bible teaching and adult fellowship in the evening. He indicated that there are several other adult teachers and workers who do not have the opportunity of attending, such as general officers and secretaries.

A woman across the street from the church who attends another church in the mornings, comes because of the excellent Bible study given in the evening. It is a worthwhile idea. Consider the possibilities.

35. Refrigerator Notes

Wanda Hicks, outreach leader for First Baptist Church, Chattanooga, Tennessee, prepares a publication the first Sunday of each month designed for young married couples in Sunday School, and distributes it to all those attending the departmental opening. Sunday School members who are absent, along with the department prospects, are mailed copies. The newsletter facilitates communication and participation. It provides a vehicle for recognition (new members, achievements, and prospects).

It is an introduction to Sunday School so that when prospects are telephoned the caller doesn't need to explain everything like event details such as times, places, and so forth. Many times the caller can just say, "Do you need a ride to the activity or the event of this week?"

The newsletter format is 8½ x 11-inch colored paper with print on both sides: "news" stories and features are on the front side and a calendar of events is on the back. It is suitable for posting on a refrigerator with a magnet.

36. The Anniversary Class

In March 1987, University Baptist Church in Baton Rouge, Louisiana, celebrated its fortieth anniversary. In conjunction with the month of celebration, the Sunday School started an anniversary class for people who were 55 and older. They targeted prospects from the membership roll that were born in 1932 or earlier and not presently enrolled in a Sunday School. A letter from the pastor was sent to all of these people, inviting them to come to the class. By June, the average attendance was over ten. In October, this class became a regular class with a new teacher. The idea of creating a new class every year at anniversary time is splendid. *Thanks, Gary Froelich.*

37. Contact Bible Markers

Create contact Bible Bookmarks by cutting 1½ x 8-inch strips of colored poster board. On each strip, write the name and phone number of one class member. Make a contact Bible bookmark for each member. Cover the strip with clear, adhesive paper to make the bookmark more durable. Have your Sunday School class place their bookmarks in a hat. Then let them draw out a bookmark. They are to pray for and phone that person each week for four weeks. At the end of the four-week period the bookmarks are brought back to class, and a new drawing takes place. *Paster Ron Wilcoxson from Brickwood Baptist Church, Lawrenceville, Georgia, created this idea and used it very effectively.* This was used in his pastor class and indicated that the contacts doubled. Thus, the bookmarks helped increase attendance.

38. "Finals Friends"
(An Outreach to College Students
Away from Home)

1. Obtain names, addresses, and phone numbers of college students living in the dorms. Distribute on 3 x 5 cards, one or two pairs of people, preferably young adults.

2. Two weeks before final exams, phone the students whose names you have.

3. Your conversation should include who you are and an explanation of why you want to stop by during finals to provide them with their favorite food. Find out what they want or like. Set a date and time to meet with them and deliver the food.

4. On the date, be prompt. Deliver your gift of food and pray with them for the exams coming up. Meet their roommates also and invite them to Sunday School. Then leave promptly.

5. College students appreciate this kind of caring and respond well. *Thank you, Carol Deel, Olivet Baptist Church, Honolulu, Hawaii, for this great growth idea.*

39. Letter of New Sunday School Members

Ray Moss, associate pastor of Program Ministries at Two Rivers Baptist Church in Nashville, Tennessee, sends a letter every Monday to the teachers with the names of people

who joined the church the previous Sunday or Wednesday.
The letter opens with the address to the teacher and reads
as follows:

> Dear Teacher:
> Listed below are the names and addresses of new mem-
> bers who joined our church. They are now members of your
> Bible study class. You need not fill out an enrollment slip.
> It is important that you call them before next Sunday in
> a spirit of love, positiveness, and enthusiasm, welcoming
> them to your class. Share information about yourself,
> where your class meets, and so forth.
> Should they prefer a different class, ask them to go by the
> Visitor Center and register for the class of their choice or
> call me, and I'll give them personal assistance.
> I know we have a mutual desire for every church mem-
> ber to be active in Bible study. Thank you for your leader-
> ship and initiative in reaching these new people for your
> class.
>
> In Christ,
> Ray Moss

At the bottom of the page, list the names of new members. Addresses and phone numbers are listed for the teacher's benefit, also. This covers the possibility of a teacher not
being aware that a new person has joined the class. Plus, it
gives new people immediate awareness of where they can
attend Sunday School. Yet it gives them the freedom to
change classes if necessary.

40. Medical Profession Day

*Verlon Moore, pastor of Hilldale Baptist Church in
Clarksville, Tennessee, shared this successful idea which he*

plans to use each year to recognize the medical personnel in his town.

Not only did Moore recognize the medical profession, but a personal letter went to each physician in the city, and it read as follows:

Dear Doctor:

You in the healing arts are special people! Since you are special to the community and to the people of Hilldale Baptist Church, we want to honor you and recognize you.

We are having "Medical Profession Day" on April 23 at Hilldale. We will have a carnation for you to wear, and we will attempt to make you feel great about your profession. We will provide a table for you to display your office brochures. This will give our people an opportunity to get to know what services are available in Clarksville. You may stand by your display after the service to give people an opportunity to get to know you, and maybe you could answer questions about medical careers that our youth might have.

Thank you for all you do for others. We are looking forward to this opportunity to get to know you. Please respond by letter so that we can set up a table for your office and make proper plans to honor you.

Gratefully yours,
Verlon Moore, Pastor

A personal letter from the pastor to other medical persons read as follows:

Dear Medical Person:

We are going to have "Medical Profession Day" the first Sunday of next month at Hilldale. We are going to have medical guests in our 10 AM service.

I will have a red carnation for all of you. Will you please wear your "uniform"? Also, if you would like, bring some brochures from your office to display in our foyer.
I am counting on you to make this day a success.

Gratefully yours,
Verlon Moore

The pastor stated the great joy of his people and the medical profession that they experienced on this particular day. A personal letter came from one of the leading doctors of the city in reconstructive surgery, and he wrote:

Dear Brother Moore:
I enjoyed very much participating in your "Medical Profession Day" at Hilldale. I felt quite honored by your asking me to participate by your public recognition of my participation. I was pleased to be able to meet you, your staff, and members of your congregation. It was indeed an honor to be with you all.

Sincerely,
Dr. Harry S. Creekmore, MD

Moore indicated that "the most important outcome was that it allowed our church to know the doctors, technicians, and nurses in the congregation. Two lives have been saved by our doctors and nurses at church functions. For that we are greatly appreciative. Our people were not aware how many people in the congregation were connected with the medical profession. To send out all the letters, we used the telephone book to locate addresses." Moore also expressed the feeling that the medical profession is often an "unwitnessed-to" group of people. Many in the congregation stated that they were grateful for this opportunity.

41. Key Chain Contact

Inreach is just as important as outreach. Therefore, a simple daily reminder is needed to do the job effectively.

Distribute key chains to class members with a blank card in a plastic holder to write the individual's name. These can be acquired from a novelty house.

Ask each class member to write his/her name and phone number on one side of the card. In one corner of that side of the card write the initial M. Circle the M. This indicates a class member.

Turn the card over, choose a prospect's name from the class prospect file. (Lead the class to choose different names.) Write the name and phone number on the reverse side of the card. In a corner of the card write the initial P. Circle the P. This indicates a prospect for the class.

Place the card in the plastic holder. Now trade with a fellow class member.

Each class member now has a fellow class member's name and phone number and a prospect's name and number.

Encourage the class to pray for the two names on the key ring—just a short breath of a prayer as they see the name on the key ring in daily activities.

Contact the fellow member and prospect by phone or when you see them, telling them you prayed for them. Encourage them. Ask them to be in Sunday School next Sunday. This is a bona fide contact.

Attaching the key ring to their personal set of keys helps as a daily reminder. This becomes an evangelistic life-style activity. Each month trade key rings to pray for two other people.

Thank you, Donald Allen, of Exchange Avenue Baptist Church, Oklahoma City, Oklahoma.

42. Reclaiming Chronic Absentees

Reclaiming chronic absentees is a problem in most churches. *The following has been a proven method in Gary Stanton's ministry in Kansas City, MO.*

Week One: Pray for all the persons you want to reach by name in each Sunday School class. Assign each active member one or more names they will pray for by name daily. Make a prayer list poster for each class to be put up and kept up to date with daily information.

Week Two: Pray (same as week one).

Week Three: Pray (same as week one).

Week Four: Pray (same as week one).

Week Five: Begin your contacts. Each member should make contact by telephone to his or her assigned person. They should continue to pray daily for this person.

Week Six: The person assigned the name should make a second contact by telephone. Continue to pray daily.

Week Seven: The person assigned the name should make the third contact in person. This shows a caring attitude.

Week Eight: Reassign names in order to change contact persons. Each person takes three new persons and contacts them by telephone.

Week Nine: The contact person now contacts by card or letter. As you can see, this makes five times the absentee or prospect has been contacted by letter, phone, or in person.

Week Ten: The contact person should visit at this time.

Week Eleven: Reassign absentees or prospects and repeat the process for the third time. Begin with a phone call.

Week Twelve: The contact person should send a card or letter.

Week Thirteen: The contact person should now visit.

As you can see, each person to be contacted is first and foremost prayed for by name once a week for seven weeks by the Sunday School class. In addition to that the same person is being prayed for individually daily for thirteen weeks. Furthermore the person receives three phone calls or more, three cards and three visits, by three different people in a thirteen-week span. This program has been used, and studies have shown a 70 percent success rate when followed as outlined. The reason for this has been prayer. It is and always will be the most powerful way we have of reaching people for Christ.

In order for this plan to be effective, the involvement of the Sunday School leadership, especially an outreach team, is essential. The outreach team (Sunday School Class) working with the plans director (which may well be the Sunday School Director) who is responsible for overseeing the coordination of the plan, the training of the workers, and the implementation of all actions.

The unique aspect of this plan is that a church can bend it to fit any target group it desires, such as new homeowners, church visitors, and those already mentioned.

If we are to grow as churches, it is important that we show we *care* for those who are already on our rolls, as well as those whom we are trying to reach. Be a church that cares by *Living a Life Worth Sharing and Sharing a Life Worth Living.*

4
Outreach and Visitation Ideas for Growth

43. Reserved Parking for Visitors

Dick Baker, pastor of First Baptist Church, Duluth, Georgia, has led his church to have half a dozen parking places for visitors who generally come to the 11:00 AM hour or possibly even after the services have begun. Many times church parking lots are filled, and the inconvenience of finding a vacancy sometimes is annoying. He told the following story: "A man and his wife, along with their two children, had been visiting a number of churches in the area. One Sunday they came to First Baptist Church. When they arrived, the parking lot was crowded. What a pleasant surprise to find a parking place, not only convenient to the main auditorium, but these were actually reserved for visitors."

As one result the family moved their letter to First Baptist Church that morning. The father of the family said, "Reserved parking for visitors does pay off." He encourages all churches to have an area designated for visitors.

44. Spring Warm-Up

The story of the Ethiopian eunuch who posed the question, "How can I understand unless someone explains it to me?" is still true today. Bible Study/Sunday School is an apropos place to grasp the truth of God's Word. Spring warm-up for growth is an opportunity to enlist people in bringing others so they may understand God's plan for their lives. James 4:2 states, "You have not because you ask not."

During the seven-week emphasis, the Sunday School is divided into teams for the *Spring Warm-Up* by scoring points and runs much like baseball. The Sunday School departments are divided into teams and compete against each other. Each week's emphasis is made on four different types of contacts such as visits to prospects, four points; visits to members, three points; phone calls to prospects, three points; to members, two points; letters and cards to prospects, two points; members, one point. A new member enrolled nets ten points. At the close of the Spring Warm-Up, scores are totaled to discover the winning team and the most valuable player.

An appreciation banquet should be held at the close of the emphasis. Fifteen gift certificates may be awarded. A plaque designed to be used for ten years may be given. *Gary Ball pastors the small Friendship Baptist Church, in Coon Rapids, Minnesota.* When the emphasis was started there were forty-nine enrolled in Sunday School with twenty-three average attendance and five contacts being made each week. At the close of the emphasis, they had seventy enrolled, with thirty-nine in attendance and an average of thirty contacts made each week. This idea can be used and adapted by any size church.

45. How to Put "POW" into Visitation

Certain times of the year visitation takes a bit of a dip or hits a slump. Here is how to put "POW" into visitation during those periods, *Prospect of the Week.*

From Thanksgiving until Valentine's Day, emphasis on visitation outreach programs sometimes takes a backseat. This idea is to "lift up" the visitation and outreach program. Each class focuses on a prospect and makes an effort to reach one prospect and enroll him or her in Sunday School. This is also true in the Preschool and Children's Departments, making the emphasis toward an individual instead of the class going after several prospects.

Using this emphasis during those periods of time prevents the visitation from dropping into the doldrums. It helps to indicate who has the prospect's name and who the prospect is. This gives the secretary or outreach director a record of what's happening. The "POW" name is selected from a list of recent visitors to the Sunday School and/or worship services. This gives high priority to the person and follow through for the latest prospects. The prospect information is entered on an outreach prospect assignment card. Regular visitation is continued until the person joins the Sunday School class.

The special emphasis of reaching preschool and older children of the Sunday School and the possibilities of reaching an entire family give variety to the program.

The "POW" prospects idea was started by *Kay Moebes of Central Baptist Church, Decatur, Alabama.*

46. Journey of Love

This is a five-week program that can be conducted in spring or fall. Ideally, it is best to plan the program to be completed on Easter Sunday. The fifth week before Easter could be entitled "Love in Deed." During this week do a little something for someone who does not expect it. Bake a cake, mow the lawn, iron some clothes, run some errands, or choose a small gift for that person.

The fourth week can be entitled "Love in Writing." This week, write a note or letter to three people, expressing your gratitude and love for them. If you are married, leave a surprise note for your mate somewhere he or she will be sure to find it. Perhaps write a note to an elderly person you admire.

In the third week, emphasize "Love in Speech." Go to someone and verbally express what they have meant to you. Call someone you care for and pray with them over the phone. Seize every opportunity to tell people how much they mean to you.

During the second week, "Love in a Meal," ask several people over for lunch or dinner. Serve the meal by expressing the purpose when you extend the invitation. Let conversations develop naturally. The meal can be a time of true fellowship.

The week before Easter could be called "Love Through a Journey." That week go out of doors either with a friend or with your spouse and family. Listen to the sounds. What do you hear? Feel the bark of a tree. Put your hand into a stream, smell flowers, walk in the woods, and skip along with your children. Become more aware of the beauty of life. Experience it through your senses.

The week of Easter can be called "Loving Prayer and Praise." Spend time alone in prayer. Try to construct a visual image in your mind of Christ on the cross. Imagine how He agonized, how He felt. Read through the last words of Christ. Repeat them aloud and look up as you pray. Seek to envision the agony Christ knew as He became God's provision for our sins. Thank Him for it.

On Easter Sunday, gather together, rejoice, and celebrate the new birth. Bring an unsaved person to church with you. Anytime throughout the day when someone says to you, "He is risen," respond by saying, "He is risen indeed!" *Thanks to Windy Rich, Nashville, Tennessee, for this great five-week emphasis on love.*

47. A Garden of New Christians

Gardens do not grow by themselves. Neither do Sunday School classes. Compare the two and see what it takes to grow a garden of new Christians.

Gathering seeds. Obtain your seeds from any of the following possible sources: church visitors, Sunday School visitors, family members of church or Sunday School members, Vacation Bible School records, personal friends, neighbors, business acquaintances, and persons who provide you with services or products.

Ground breaking. The first visit is not likely to produce a new member or a new Christian. It is a time to become acquainted and express a desire to have future contact. It is a time to show initial concern.

Planting. Begin with the first visit to give your testimony and invite the prospect to Sunday School. Offer as much witness as the prospect will accept with interest. Sometimes this may not be much, but always offer.

Watering. Get to know your chosen prospects. Visit together often. Invite them over for a party or a meal.

Cultivating. Be sure your class and circle of friends are always open to receive another member. Have the class outreach leader assign people to a group so that friendship will be cultivated. The prospects will become group members when they join the Sunday School class.

Harvesting. Present the plan of salvation and ask for a decision. Every gardener knows he has to pick the fruits of his labor. If the prospects say no, go back to cultivating and ask again at a later time. Don't become discouraged. Don't quit trying. When prospects say yes, remember your job has just begun. Help them to become true disciples of Christ by encouraging them to study the Bible, both at home and in Sunday School. Show them how to pray and encourage them to pray. Include them in your efforts to win other souls to Christ and help them to begin to grow a garden of new Christians for themselves.

This idea came from Dr. Tommy Stevens, pastor of Allen Baptist Church, Brownsville, Tennessee.

48. Outreach Express

Charles Westbrook of East Bay Missionary Baptist Church, Riverview, Florida, created this idea of dividing the Sunday School into equal groups, forming a train. Behind the "engine" are different cars for phone calls, door knocking, and cards and letters.

The last train car is the caboose, which is the number of people enrolled during the fourteen-week emphasis. Points are given for each contact and added up at the end of the period. Each team member wears a name tag indicating which outreach train car they are on.

A song is composed and sung throughout the competition. An appreciation banquet is given at the end of the quarter, recognizing the various "trains" and the "loads" they carried. It can be a success. At East Bay the enrollment increased from 215 to 257. The attendance rose from an average of 70 to 109. Obviously the train delivered a precious cargo at the end of the period.

49. Outreach on Christmas Eve

Serving as chaplain in residence at the state psychiatric hospital in Mandeville, Louisiana, was a unique situation, says Lynne Scott of First Baptist Church, Newnan, Georgia. The clinical director, Dr. Adrian Dean, is an ordained Baptist minister/psychiatrist who had incorporated worship services into the hospital's treatment schedule.

"A part of my responsibility as chaplain for Protestant patients in this 450-bed hospital was to lead Tuesday night and Sunday-morning worship," testified Dr. Dean. "I began to consider how local community churches could become involved in this work. There was already a group of men coming on Tuesday, once a month, but they lived fifty miles away. Local churches were not connected with the hospital. This was understandable in the traditional sense of how most people view psychiatric facilities—especially state ones. But there is one thing isolated, lonely, wounded people need—and that is community. Experience has taught that the foundation of any new project is the relationship between/among God's people. Trust is generally higher among the familiar."

Scott went to the church where she had become a member—First Baptist Church of Mandeville—and spoke to the pastor, Bob Ferguson, who is a twenty-year veteran missionary to Germany who had returned to the states. He was new and open to ministry options close by. He agreed to take the lead, initially.

"Under Ferguson's guided discipline, he began to bring

people out to worship with us at the hospital—first the staff, then several deacons, and then youth groups," continued Scott. "The ladies of the church provided food for fellowship one Tuesday evening (a big turnout of Catholics to a Protestant service that night). Eventually, one deacon with a heart for life's wounded people took the lead and began to conduct the services. The pastor still came, but the deacon led. There were many questions asked, some answered. The attitude toward all who came was one of welcome and opennesss to God's Spirit to guide them in deciding if this was the ministry situation for them. Everyone learned that the greatest 'idea' is human relationships shared in the spirit of Christ's love.

"A most vivid picture was on Christmas Eve, 1987. First Baptist Church, Mandeville, held its annual Christmas Eve candlelight Lord's Supper service. The church extended an invitation to bring fifty patients (all ages—five to senior adults) to participate."

With much cooperation and Christmas love, arrangements were made for patients chosen by their doctors to attend off-ground services. In a psychiatric setting, this is most unusual. As often happens, there was an unexpected mix-up—the church changed the service time. The group arrived thirty minutes late. The church was packed.

"We had fifty excited psychiatric patients wanting desperately to be a part," noted Scott. "The Lord's Supper was served, family style, with people going to the tables in the front to take the meal together in a family group. As we entered the church, a most amazing thing happened. The beautiful First Baptist Church people opened spaces all around the auditorium and placed the people from the hospital among them. No one was on the periphery. Everyone was wrapped in one another's arms.

"There were those who had not felt safe and welcome in a church in years. On that special night, God's children knew Jesus would not have sent anyone away."

Outreach Ministry is to *all* of God's People.

50. Good Neighbors, Friends, School, Business

This idea has to do with outreach visitation and finding prospects. *It is shared with us by T. D. McCulloch of Texarkana, Texas, retired director of missions.*

1. *Being a Good Neighbor:* Enlist wives and senior adults who do not work away from home to be "good neighbors."

a. Watch for moving vans and U-Hauls. When one is spotted moving into a house on your street, go to the house with iced tea or coffee and a cake or pie from the deep-freeze for a brief, friendly visit telling them how glad you are they are moving into the neighborhood. Gather as much information as you can from the visit and call the church, if it sounds as if they are prospects.

b. Make cultivator fellowship contacts or brief good-neighbor contacts to win their friendship and respect.

c. Keep a zip-lock of printed materials and tracts to use. If a "good neighbor" misses a prospect and the church gets the name from another source, the information on a card should be sent to the good neighbor so he can begin to develop a relationship and possibly enlist them.

These good neighbors need not be deacons or Sunday School workers. They could be just members of classes and drop in from time to time to make a visit.

2. *Friends at Work:* This is an excellent way to find prospects, and it works the same as "good neighbors." They look for prospects at work and use coffee breaks or lunch hours as a time to cultivate witness and enlistment for the Sunday School.

3. *Friends at School:* Works the same as the above two. Children and youth who make a special effort to be friends with new students at school can bring many of these prospects to Sunday School and other church activities. They also can call the names of prospects they find for the church and send them a card to look up those that they may have missed. Children and youth workers can organize this approach in their departments.

4. *Business Friends:* Church members in the business world (real estate, medicine, banking, utilities, and so forth) are in a good position to meet a number of people and invite many of their business associates to Sunday School. Each prospect found is called from the office or information is dropped on a card to the church office.

These as well as staff members, deacons, Sunday School workers, and other trained witnesses should keep a zip-lock bag of material in their cars ready for use when they talk to prospects.

The church may want to use a learning module on witnessing, which is excellent, and can be used as an ongoing study until all deacons, Sunday School workers, and a large portion of members are effective witnesses. Don't forget the use of organized units in the Sunday School and causing them to function properly.

Adult classes with more small groups of four and five members can minister to a member and have time to cultivate and bring prospects. It helps considerably that the class officers keep a packet size "prayer and prospect book." Use it nightly to pray for the members and prospects and daily to make opportunities to contact these people as they come and go in the community.

Each member keeps a record of his contacts and ministry and reports them by phone to the group leaders or the outreach leader. This way the information can be shared in the class on either Wednesday night, visitation night, or Sunday morning. In the Sunday morning classes, the outreach leader can give a brief highlight of what is happening in the contacting of the class prospects. It takes the right kind of enlistment and training for officers to do the job most effectively.

Some Sunday School directors can from time to time meet with new outreach leaders for training and receive words of encouragement from the minister of education and pastor. A checkup period occasionally needs to be done with information shared with the pastor. The Sunday School director can share unusual activities and experiences that some of the visitors are having.

There is the need for a constant follow through from the church staff and Sunday School director to the outreach leaders to make the plan work most effectively and efficiently.

51. Compound the Contacts

The youth of the First Baptist Church, Glendale, Arizona, make the most of visitation, according to Phil Burgman, the minister of education. Here is how it works.

Two youths choose the name of an enrolled Sunday School member who has been absent for a while. On visita-

tion night they go see that absentee member. Then they go
to the house next door. They knock on the door. When the
homeowner answers the door, the youth explain, "We're visiting _____ your next door neighbor. We're from
_____ Church and wanted to find out if you're attending Sunday School anywhere. We'd like to invite you to our
class." If the person is not attending the question is asked,
"Could we enroll you?" Some prospects will be enrolled.
Sometimes the youth also find other members of the family
who are not attending.

Since they are in the neighborhood they use the same
approach to both sides of the house of the absentee youth
and across the street, finding prospects for their Sunday
School class and other departments of the Sunday School.
This idea saves time in travel as the youth go to one location, park their car, and perhaps knock on the doors of four
or five houses in one stop. If the absentee does not happen
to be at home they are still able to make other contacts and
not come back to the church empty-handed.

Burgman said this type of "prospect hunt" has been most
effective, and the youth enjoy it. Some try to see how many
doors they can knock on in one evening.

5
Enrollment Ideas for Growth

52. Prospect Harvest

James E. Harvey of the Baptist Sunday School Board has the responsibility of January Bible Study material. He said, "I've collected a number of prospects who have visited my Sunday School class during the last six months. I discovered that nineteen of these people resided in the immediate community of the church. I decided I would sit down one Sunday afternoon and give these prospects a phone call, asking them if I could enroll them in Sunday School. I was surprised that I enrolled all nineteen of them! Not one said no."

Keep in mind James 4:2, "Ye have not, because ye ask not." Many people are ready to join a class if we ask them.

53. Subdivision Visitation

This idea is an ongoing visitation program to update information in subdivisions. On a special visitation night, visitors go to a particular home with the idea of seeing the people who live at the address. However, it is also the intent to visit the people to the right and to the left of the given address, even though they do not have information about the people.

While visiting the prospect they find out basic information about who lives next door—the number of children, church home, and other pertinent data.

Church workers have discovered that new prospects are gained but also newcomers welcomed the visit from the church in their community. This maximizes the effectiveness of going out because many times the prospect will not be at home. At least there is the opportunity to make two other calls, one on each side of the house where you are going to visit. *"If that fails, you always have the other side of the street," remarked Sid Hopkins, director of missions in the Lawrenceville Association, Lawrenceville, Georgia.* The idea helped a small church to become one of the largest churches in the association.

Records were kept of the visits. Within a short period of time a complete survey was made of the entire subdivision. The survey was constantly updated when people would move. A visitor on visitation night could easily contact three to four homes in a hour and a half or two hours. When a person was not at home, a door hanger with identification of the church (address, phone number, pastor's name, and visitor's name) was left on the door. On the reverse side of the door hanger was a map of the entire church community that included a number of subdivisions, showing roads leading to *the Atkinson Road Baptist Church where Sid was pastor at that time.*

54. Double Vision

Ordinarily double vision refers to a real problem. However, a vision of doubling the entire Sunday School enrollment in one year can be a genuine vision of joy. *Rosedale Baptist Church, Abingdon, Virginia, under the skillful leadership of Jimmy Cox, pastor, decided to have double vision and go for double enrollment.*

The campaign started with 179 people enrolled the first of October. The open enrollment concept was used. Teachers were encouraged not to drop anyone unless they moved, joined another church, or died. They made every effort to enroll anyone and everyone who would join the first time they came to Sunday School. Their target groups were church members not enrolled, parents of children not enrolled, and others who were not attending elsewhere. The first quarter meant a goal of 201. By the end of December they had enrolled 209. The next quarter the goal was to reach an enrollment of 223. By the end of that time, the second quarter, they had enrolled 242. At the end of the first year the enrollment was to be 268. They missed it! They went over the goal. The actual enrollment reached was 272.

Like most programs the church was concerned about the attendance and somewhat skeptical whether the attendance would hold in the same ratios. The Sunday School director, C. W. Price, believed in the plan. To their joy and surprise the attendance moved from 130 to 211 on Easter, which surpassed any of their wildest dreams. The sanctuary was completely filled and many people had to sit in the balcony.

As part of the goal, the last Sunday of every quarter was high attendance Sunday which was reached and surpassed each month. The church is still pressing toward increasing the enrollment and carrying on the double vision. At last count the Sunday School had 358 enrolled with 268 present. Pastor Cox's comment was, "To God be the glory!"

55. Pastor Enrolls People from the Pulpit

Don Hull, minister of education of Fielder Road Baptist Church in Arlington, Texas, indicates his pastor has started a new practice of literally enrolling people from the pulpit. He attempts to enroll visitors who are there for the worship hour who do not attend Sunday School anywhere.

He was elated the first Sunday he attempted the idea as he enrolled twenty-five people on his first try. The second Sunday he enrolled thirty-two people, and the third Sunday, twenty-nine. In five months he enrolled a total of 225 people. This is more in five months than the church had shown in the past two Sunday School years.

Your gain may not be that great, but whatever it is, it can be a tremendous increase and will establish a mind-set for the leadership of the Sunday School to think enrollment as their pastor does. It certainly keeps a lot of visitors from "slipping through your fingers," and never being asked to be a part of the total church program.

56. Bulletin "Flap" Pays Off

Many churches print the worship hour bulletins on 8½ x 11″ sheets of paper. Consider printing the bulletin on a legal-size sheet which gives you a foldover flap of approximately 2½ inches by 8½.

On one side of the flap promote the Sunday School from the pulpit. Give a simple outline of next Sunday's Sunday School lesson. The text is given and a list of three to five questions concerning next Sunday's lesson are given with space to fill in the blanks. The paragraph under the text might read: "When you study next Sunday's lesson, look for the answers to the following questions." Then list 1, 2, 3, 4, 5. At the bottom quote 2 Timothy 2:15: "Study to show thyself approved unto God . . ."

On the flip side of the "flap" put the heading in capital letters: BE A MEMBER OF SUNDAY SCHOOL. Underneath print two words, Enroll Me. Have lines for a person to write his name, address, city, zip, phone number, and birthday.

It may be easier to make the Sunday School information flap parallel with the 8½ x 11 ″ length of the sheet, leaving lines where a person can write in name, address, city, zip, phone number, birthday, and then put in parentheses: (Fill out and place in the offering plate.)

Obviously this does several things: It indicates the pastor is for the Sunday School. It gives opportunity for people who are either visitors or church members not enrolled to be enrolled—plus it encourages all those in attendance to prepare for next Sunday's lesson.

57. Checkbook Enrollment

Enrollment slips are made in a checkbook format (show the printer a check on the local bank with the stub to the left of the check. You may have to adapt a little at this point).

Sunday School members carry the checkbook with them all the time, much like they do with their own personal checkbook. When they meet a person who could be enrolled in Sunday School, they ask the question, "Could I enroll you in our Sunday School?" If the person says yes, fill out the enrollment check and give it to the new enrollee. Fill out the stub and turn it in to the church office.

On the stub have the following information: the date. On the check have a blank place to insert the date, name of enrollee address and phone.

The church may offer a welcome gift to the individual when they "cash" in their check at the church office or welcome desk of the Sunday School. The gift from the church could be a copy of the New Testament, a Bible bookmark, or some other comparable memento.

"This idea is very effective," states the executive director of Southern Baptists of Arizona, Dr. Jack Johnson.

58. GET

I like acrostics and alliteration. The acrostic GET stands for "Grandparents Enrolling Tots." *Tim Gentry, pastor of the West Roseville Baptist Church in Roseville, California, gave us this idea.*

Many emphases are made on enrolling people in Sunday School, but most of the time the emphasis is toward enrolling youth and adults, and few ideas seek small children except for the Cradle Roll. GET gives us this opportunity of seeking small children. Therefore, in the main auditorium or in classes or departments where there are grandparents, circulate a 3 x 5 card to all attenders, and ask them to list all of their grandchildren who live in the church community who are not attending Sunday School anywhere. List address, phone number, age, and other pertinent information. Some of these can be enrolled by telephone, post cards, or a prospect card filled out and given to the proper age-group department.

Thanks, Tim, for this GRAND-parent idea. Let's GET them!

59. "Break the Ice"

This idea comes from Gary Johnson, Vale Baptist Church, Bloomington, Illinois. It is an idea that might be used during the fall or winter seasons and he called, "Break the Ice."

It is an outreach/visitation campaign to be used during one quarter. Implement the idea one month rotating the special emphasis each week for two or three months depending on when the program is started. For example, October and November could be used very satisfactorily, or February and March would be good also. The idea is designed to develop personal friendships with people at work, neighbors, and church prospects. This may not produce immediate results, but on the long run they should be lasting results. Emphasis is placed on using the regular visitation night or when a person can make his or her contacts. However, another night might have to be used when scheduling events.

Make a Friend—During the first week, contact a prospect from the Sunday School file in the age-group of your class or department. During that period of time you may want to spend some time with them. Do not be in a hurry to leave when you visit. As you find out what their interests are, try to match someone else in the class that may have a similar interest for them to be contacted in the future. The two people will then have some similar interests.

Cake a Friend—During the second week, invite a friend to your home for coffee and cake. Perhaps this friend could be a neighbor or business associate or someone else you happen to be interested in. This works well with church prospects. It is best to invite only one family at a time. This allows for more personal conversation.

Wake a Friend—During the third week, contact a friend you haven't seen in awhile. Surprise him with a visit. Renew your relationship. This gives you an excellent opportunity to invite them to church! This week might also be used in matching prospects from the first week's visit.

Take a Friend—During the fourth week, take a friend to a ball game, the gym, or to a community activity. Once again this might be a neighbor, business associate, or a church prospect. In a casual manner you are developing a friendship. You will be able to share your faith in a natural way.

Shake a Friend—During the fifth week, have everyone come to church early for prayer. Invite other people to come pray as people go in with one of their friends they have been contacting. The intention of this is to share Christ with each friend.

On the following Sunday conduct a special service. This is not intended as a high attendance campaign. The emphasis on that Sunday should be a clear presentation of the gospel. A suggested Scripture might be Matthew 5:16, "Let your light so shine before men, that they may see your good works, and glorify your Father which is in heaven."

60. Everyone Welcome Envelope

One of the most fascinating envelopes I've seen is from First Baptist Church of Tucker, Georgia. Using the #10 envelope, it has the name and address of the church perpendicular on the left-hand edge. Then in very small print are the names of various occupations. They are listed on lines about three and one-half inches wide horizontally on the left side. There are forty-eight lines of various occupations. Allow me to read the first three lines: artist, auctioneer, accountant, banker, butcher, teller, clerk, barber, carpenter, cook, cashier, dentist, lawyer, guard, flight attendant, librarian, musician, doctor, painter, photographer, surveyor, police officer, plumber, programmer, roofer, nurse, broker.

Then cut out and use white space on five lines that are overlaid over all of the printing. The five lines read:

First line: "No matter who you are"
Second line: "You need what"
Third line: "We have at First Baptist"
Fourth line: "And we would like to"
Fifth line: "Share it with you."

It catches the eye and gives one a feeling of: "There's a place for me and they're interested."

6
High Attendance Ideas for Growth

61. "Let Your Light Shine"— High Attendance Day

Suggested time of year: spring or holiday season

Verse for the campaign: Matthew 5:16: "Let your light shine before . . ."

Symbol for the campaign publicity: a lighthouse

Thrust of the day: Every person in Sunday School makes a commitment to turn on his light by their attendance (strings of tiny Christmas tree lights are hung from the 10-foot replica of a lighthouse).

Plans for High Attendance Day:

Fifth week before High Attendance Campaign: attendance goal is set by Sunday School workers.

Fourth week before High Attendance Day: a newsletter starts and continues each week.

Second and third weeks before High Attendance Day:

Commitment cards are passed out in Sunday School departments.

1. Individuals make a commitment to be present and sign a card.
2. A portion of the card (where the person signs his

name) is attached to individual lights on a string of Christmas tree lights.

Second week before High Attendance Day: A ten-foot replica of a lighthouse (built by a layperson) is placed in the sanctuary.

First week before High Attendance Day:

1. There is a giant visitation effort.
2. Strands of light are strung on the lighthouse (one light for each person signed up to attend).
3. Names are placed on individual lights.

High Attendance Day:

1. Attendance is announced in the service.
2. Each individual light on the string of lights is turned on (one light for each person in Bible study).
3. The light at the top of the lighthouse is lit if the attendance goal is reached.
4. The sermon can be from Matthew 5:16.

Results of the Campaign:

1. The First Baptist Church of Old Ocean, Texas, experienced the largest attendance ever. A church averaging 400 had over 600 in Sunday School.
2. Each person felt if he were not present on that day . . . the light at the top of the lighthouse would not be lit because the goal would not be reached.
3. A victorious worship service was held. Each person saw again his life as a light to shine for Christ.

A variation from the tiny Christmas lights could be to use larger old-fashioned Christmas tree lights and have each person write his name on the bulb instead of the tiny white Christmas tree lights.

This idea comes from Mike Sabo, minister of education, First Baptist Church, Old Ocean, Texas.

62. SPRING Campaign for Growth

Spiritual Principles Resulting in New Growth is the meaning of this acrostic.

SPRING is an eight-week campaign resulting in renewed emphasis on contacts, enrolling, and attendance. It culminates in a High Attendance Day on Easter Sunday.

Each class is challenged by the pastor, minister of education, and Sunday School director to earn motivational points in order to minister and to win the coveted SPRING award each week. Each class won points using the following point system:

Contacts	1 point
Enrolling new members (per member)	10 points
Weekly worker's meeting attendance	10 points
Visitation attendance (per person)	2 points
New commitments to attend Easter	5 points

The class with the highest points won each week's SPRING award, and the class with the highest points for the campaign won the Grand Prize SPRING Award: steak dinner served by the church staff. (The SPRING award was a "slinky" toy attached to an award plaque.) The campaign required one plaque per week plus an extra large one to the Grand-Prize-winning class. A letter was mailed to all Sunday School members to announce the campaign. Enclosed was a flower seed for them to plant, so they could observe God at work in nature. Causing the flower to grow and attending Sunday School, they could observe Sunday School work as God was at work in the membership.

Posters were used to enlist commitments to attendance and to advertise the event in every class room. Each class had commitment stickers to attach to each poster. The stickers were a means of signing up people to attend the High Attendance Day. Each poster could hold twenty such commitments. Each class set its own attendance goal which was published in the church newspaper.

This simple, but excellent, idea comes from Mike Felder, Saint Simons First Baptist Church, Saint Simons Island, Georgia. His church implemented the idea, and these were the results. Previous to the campaign the average attendance was 481. Only occasionally had it exceeded 500. A very ambitious goal of 650 was set for the attendance. At the time there were about 1,000 people enrolled in Sunday School. The result on Easter Sunday went way beyond the expectations and over the top of the goal. There were 720 in Bible study on Easter Sunday High Attendance Day.

Why and how? Because people became motivated to do the basics of Sunday School is the *why*. Contacts soared from an average of 250 to an average of 852 during the campaign. There was a total of 6,812 contacts in the eight weeks of the campaign. Fifty-one new people were enrolled. Average attendance in Sunday School during the campaign rose to 562. Five of the highest Sunday School attendances and three of the highest outreach nights attendances were reached during the campaign.

63. Thanksgiving "SAFAREE"

This acrostic means: Senior Adult Friends And Relatives Enrollment Emphasis.

The Thanksgiving Safaree has a dual purpose: First, Thanksgiving is an excellent time to recognize and express gratitude to all senior adults who have made and continue to make tremendous contributions to the churches and to the community. Second, senior adults, like everyone else, have needs to which the Sunday School can uniquely minister. They, too, need to be enrolled in a caring, ministering Sunday School which can introduce the lost to Jesus Christ and aid Christians in spiritual maturity.

Advantages to the Church

- Identifies, reclaims, challenges inactive church members
- Helps start new classes alongside established senior adult classes
- Creates an "if *they* can *grow* we can too" attitude among other adult departments
- Because the senior adults are involved in the process of preparation, visiting, and follow-up, volunteers can be identified to help in various ministries and needs around the church after the safaree is finished.
- Discovers senior adults who recently have become homebound and can now be ministered to through the Homebound Ministry

The church can enroll senior adult church members not already in Sunday School. It opens the door to evangelistic follow-up visits to some homes.

The "Thanksgiving Safaree" schedule can be similar to the following suggestions. The fourth Sunday before Thanksgiving became an emphasis called "Scouting Sunday." Use a card entitled "Track 'em Down" in the morning worship service to identify anyone who is 65 years of age or older not enrolled in Sunday School. On the third Sunday emphasize "Tracking Sunday." These senior adults are asked in each adult department to assemble and fill out the "Track 'em Down" card as to whom they will "track down." Provide an opportunity to think of other prospects overlooked the previous Sunday.

The second Sunday prior to Thanksgiving can be called "The Big Hunt." The "Big Hunt" is actually a mini-people search conducted by the senior adult Sunday School members aimed at the prospects discovered the previous Sunday. After a light lunch and brief instructions are given, each team of two receives a packet of six to eight prospects to visit, and each home visited receives a copy of *Home Life, Mature Living,* a New Testament, and a brochure about the church.

The final Sunday before Thanksgiving is "Trophy Day." A section of the main auditorium is reserved for senior adult members' seating. The front two rows are additionally reserved for those who were pre-enrolled on "The Big Hunt." Recognition is given to these people during the worship service as genuine "trophies."

After returning from "The Big Hunt," one seventy-year-old woman remarked, "We needed to do this more than anything else to show others we really care about them." Her 69-year-old partner chimed in, "Yes, and we found one of our friends who was not enrolled in Sunday School, and she is one of our faithful church members."

The pastor's comments were that the "SAFAREE" not only showed good health, but real life was manifested in the church. So often, an attitude is assumed that senior adults grow old and become feeble and shut-in. They often demonstrate that Sunday School can grow through active enlistment, not merely in the younger age groups but among the older folks as well. "Growing" senior adult classes is important, exciting, and inspiring. *Robert Lynn Park, minister of education, Fayetteville First Baptist Church, Fayetteville, Georgia, created this idea.*

64. Happy Anniversary

If your church is planning to celebrate a significant anniversary, why not use it to reach a record Sunday School attendance?

Begin six to eight weeks prior to the targeted anniversary celebration. Prepare a large cardboard birthday cake for each department. Attach a cardboard candle for each class and department, plus one for the general officers. On the flame write the teacher's name. (Teachers are the spark to make the plan effective.)

On each candle draw a square equal to the enrollment of that class. Write each class member's name on the square. Prepare an attendance commitment card that will fit the square on the candle. Set a sign-up goal for each class and department at the base of the cake. For example, the left side would read Church goal: _____ and the right-hand side of the cake at the bottom would be Department or Class goal: _____ .

About six to eight weeks before the big day, begin signing up people to attend the anniversary celebration. As they sign up, place their card on the corresponding square or have them sign their name on the candle itself.

Teachers and department directors can call attention to the display weekly by noting the progress. Contacts each week can focus on signing up the class members for the high attendance anniversary service.

Some special features should be planned for the anniversary to help motivate people to attend. Working on the plan for eight weeks gives people plenty of time to catch the spirit of excitement and plan for the high attendance day.

Dr. Odell Carpenter, pastor of First Baptist Church, Bixby, Oklahoma, shared this idea as they celebrated the 85th anniversary of their church. His remarks were: "Attendance jumped, new enrollees were added to the membership, people came to the Lord, plus a great spirit of celebration was experienced by all of the folks involved." He added, "each Sunday the *golden doorknob* award created by Dr. Gene Skelton was used to promote the class with the greatest number of contacts each week.

65. CARE
(Call and Reach Everyone)

What a delightful acrostic—call and reach everyone! *Bo Prosser and Rita Loadholt of First Baptist Church, Roswell, Georgia are the creators of this idea.* The idea is to make personal contact with every prospect and Sunday School member in a personal way for a three-month period.

Prosser uses his church mailout bulletin to promote the idea, asking all teachers and workers and class members to become *personal,* leading them to make the Bible teaching ministry of the church a caring and sharing fellowship.

He uses people's names for recognition. For example: "APRIL GAFFNEY CARE's four-year-olds had eighteen of the nineteen present, and every child received a contact. Thanks, April, and everyone who helps us set the pace."

He uses a boxed note within the bulletin. For example, "THE CARE CHALLENGE: Teachers, group leaders, class members, we challenge you to participate in "CAREing" at least once each week, using the CARE concept of contacting with a Saturday night call to each Sunday School member.

What are the *guaranteed results?* Warmth, understanding, and John 13:35.

Bo indicates this has caused the weekly attendance to jump tremendously. CARE works.

66. Roll Call Sunday

This is an idea about how to have good attendance at a revival. However, catch the concept since it may be used with a little adaptation for Sunday School. This idea works well in small churches.

The church roll is divided into six parts or sections to represent each night of the revival, Monday night through Saturday. One section of the church roll is called or read before the entire congregation on a particular night. The revival visitation is done by the teams. They encourage each church member on their assigned list to be in attendance on a specific night of the revival. This means six visitation teams being used for each night of the revival, and the group of people for their specific night work to sit in a specific section of the auditorium to be "counted" when their names on the church roll are called. They are recognized by standing up as their names are called.

The visitation teams start visiting and making contacts three weeks before the revival. On the night of the revival the section is "accounted for" by the team leader. When the name is called and the person is absent, the leader may give an account of where the person is on that evening (that can be dangerous unless handled properly).

Rev J. W. Ray, pastor of the First Baptist Church, Rattan, Oklahoma, said 79 percent of the church membership was involved in the revival and present. Seven people were baptized at the end of the revival, and Sunday School attendance increased more than 10 percent during the three months following the revival. Each church member was contacted one or more times during the time of the revival. The theme hymn each night was "When the Roll Is Called Up Yonder" which became an effective "motivator."

67. Operation 150

This idea can be used for whatever your goal is in Sunday School. *The Northside Baptist Church in Atlanta, Georgia, under the leadership of Pastor Ed C. Smith, Jr., had not reached 150 in Bible study attendance.* Therefore, beginning eleven weeks before High Attendance Day, the following steps were followed to accomplish the goal.

In the bulletin on Sunday morning a paragraph was written: "Today begins Operation 150! This is an eleven-week outreach effort to have a total of 150 people in Sunday morning Bible study on High Attendance Day. Be a part."

High Attendance Day was set for October 30. Therefore, the beginning of the campaign was in August when attendance is generally low.

Each class is instructed to pray and visit all of their members, leading them to a commitment on Sunday morning. A large poster is placed in the auditorium marking the actual attendance each Sunday, beginning at the bottom of the poster, starting with the opening date. The progress was marked each week.

Ed said, "This led to the highest attendance in our church, and new people were enrolled. It is a simple idea that can be done by any church in any area by any group of people. The theme of the campaign made promotion relatively easy."

68. Don't-Break-My-Heart Sunday

This idea is designed for high attendance on the Sunday prior to Valentine's Day. The idea starts three weeks prior to Valentine's Sunday. A large heart is drawn on red paper. Class members' names are written on the heart. The heart is cut into pieces and given to each member of the class present. It is signed the second time by the individual and placed on the poster of the heart's outline before it is cut up.

The pieces left over are assigned to various class members to make contact with the absent person so that on Valentine's Sunday his or her part of the "puzzle" can be placed in its proper location, indicating the heart is complete and unbroken with all members present.

On "Don't-Break-My-Heart Sunday," all classes with complete hearts are recognized in the main auditorium and given a box of candy as an expression of appreciation to the teachers. The idea is that contacts are made to every member of the Sunday School class, and at the same time an expression of appreciation is given to the teachers. *This idea comes from Mary Clayton, First Baptist Church, Durham, North Carolina.*

69. "So Built We the Wall"

J. A. Eddington, minister of education and administration of Sequoyah Hills Baptist Church in Tulsa, Oklahoma, reported that this emphasis ran for nine weeks from March 1 through April 26 (which was Easter Sunday). Each department and/or class was asked to set an enrollment goal for the period.

A wall of cardboard boxes was constructed, painted, and placed behind the choir seats (approximately 45-feet long and 8-feet high when completed) with a section for each age division.

Bricks were left out of each section totaling the new member goal for the age group. Each Sunday morning, the director of the department came forward at the beginning of the worship service and added a brick in the wall for each new member enrolled in the department during the past week. Each brick inserted represented a new member in Sunday School. The goals for the departments during the emphasis totaled 154 to be reached by the last Sunday to complete the wall.

In addition to the new members and the overall goal, each department had a goal of contacts for each week and a high attendance day planned for the last Sunday. The contact goal averaged 1,305 contacts per week. The last Sunday 778 people were in attendance—the third largest attendance in the history of the church.

So built we the wall!

70. High Five

During the sports seasons you will often see the players, after a great play, jump in the air and slap a hand to a teammate's hand above their heads in joy, ecstasy, and enthusiasm for the accomplishments just attained. This salute is called a "high five."

A church emphasis can be used during sports seasons of the year (now nearly all year long). During these periods of time there are generally two five-Sunday months.

Choose one five-Sunday month to be your "high five."

During this month emphasis is given on five areas of your church program.

If you are like me, you like freedom of choice. So, I'm listing six areas of emphasis that are possibilities. Choose the five you think are most important to your church. You may have another emphasis not listed. Make it one of the five.

1. Highest total *attendance* for five weeks
2. Highest total *baptisms* in five weeks
3. Highest total number of *contacts* in five weeks
4. Highest number of *new members* in five weeks
5. Highest total attendance to *workers' meeting* in five weeks
6. Highest total amount of *offering* received in five weeks

Choose five of the six. These will become the emphasis for the five weeks you choose.

Look in last year's record, or you may check the last five years of your "highs." To discover when and what your goal should be for this year's high-five record.

Make posters, banners, bulletin inserts, whatever is necessary to promote the whole quarter and especially the "High Five" month of the emphasis.

Believe me, you will break every goal you set with a "High Five" emphasis. *Thanks to Dr. Jack Johnson, executive director, Arizona Baptist Convention, Phoenix, Arizona, for this idea.*

71. Fellowship Heart

The theme for this idea is I love Sunday School. The idea is to involve more people active in inreach and outreach, to develop a closer relationship with each other, and to support each other.

The best time of the year to use this idea is the month of February (four Sundays) or back up four Sundays before

Valentine's Day. You can make the Sunday before Valentine's Day the final high attendance day by backing up four Sundays.

First Sunday: Everyone receives a lapel button that says, "I love Sunday School."

Second Sunday: Each preschooler, child, and youth receives a helium-filled balloon that is heart shaped and says, "I love Sunday School." Encourage children's departments and youth departments to make posters illustrating the theme "I love Sunday School." Display the posters in hallways leading to the main auditorium.

Third Sunday: The emphasis is on "Attend-with-a-Friend."

Final Sunday: The emphasis is high attendance. Bring a friend and enroll him or her in Sunday School.

Jeff Hicks, minister of education at Gardenside Baptist Church in Lexington, Kentucky, created this idea. His Sunday School leaders set a goal of 701 for high attendance. Needless to say, they went over the top! Because of the "I Love Sunday School" emphasis, they averaged forty-eight higher in attendance in February of 1989 than the attendance for the previous February.

72. Back to School—"Apple Up"

Lewis Bratton, minister of activities and adults at Highland Baptist Church in Florence, Alabama, says the following idea is best to work in the month of August. High attendance day for children and youth is in late August. (If your schools start the first week in September adjust accordingly.)

The first week of August cards are sent to all grade school and high school students. If you are in a college town you may want to include college age. The card states as follows:

BACK TO SCHOOL
An apple for the teacher?????
Apples are usually given by the pupil to the teacher but not this time! On Sunday, August _____ (last Sunday of August), "Back to School High Attendance Day," your Sunday School teacher will give each person present an apple. Let's apple-up.
Count me present!!

_____
(signature)
**Please return your card to your teacher
on Sunday, August _____.**

The above card is sent to each class member with the expectation they will return the card to the teacher. This helps to approximate how many apples will be needed.

The third week the following reminder is sent to *all* the class members.

BACK TO SCHOOL
(High Attendance in Sunday School)
APPLE-UP
Pick Up Your Apple
Sunday, August _____
By Being Present
in Sunday School

The results?—The highest attendance in children and youth departments on the third and fourth Sunday in August in a number of years.

7
Summer Slump Ideas for Growth

73. 10 out of 13

This idea will encourage Sunday School attendance through the summer months. The whole concept is to attend ten of the thirteen Sundays and be a part of supporting your church during the summer months.

A 3 x 5 card with a title "10 out of 13" is distributed throughout the Sunday School classes and/or the main auditorium at the beginning of the summer months. It reads as follows:

10 out of 13

"In an effort to keep our Bible teaching program on a high plane in attendance and efficiency this summer, *I promise, God helping me, to be present at least ten Sundays out of thirteen for the summer period at the* _____ (name of your church)

Name _____

Class _____

Department _____

This has helped many churches in attendance through the summer.

74. The Summer for the Savior

When Dr. L. L. Morriss was pastor of First Baptist Church, Midland, Texas, he sent a personal letter to each member. The letter was as follows:

Dear Friend:

Here is your "Summer for the Savior" record card. Help make the summer the most spiritual time of your life. You will experience real pleasure in keeping your own record. Thank you for your loyalty during the summer months.

Sincerely yours,

L. L. Morriss

Enclosed in the letter was a card folded in half that has on the inside fold a place to keep a record of the individual's attendance in Sunday School, morning worship, evening worship, Wednesday night services, and other activities for all three months—June, July, August. A little box is provided for each week of the month for the various services. The card easily fits within an individual's Bible. The member places a checkmark in the box corresponding to the service he/she attended.

At the close of the summer, Bible bookmarks made of ribbon with the church's name and the services the person attended are presented. The ribbons are of various colors to indicate where the person was perfect in attendance.

This method of the "Summer for the Savior" attendance program was created by Bill Bumpas, minister of activities at the time. The Scripture theme for the emphasis was: "Remember the Sabbath day to keep it holy" (Ex. 20:8).

At the bottom of the card was a place for a person to sign their name and address.

This method, according to Bill, of each individual keeping their own record motivated weekly the people to attend all the services which gave an over-all emphasis of higher attendance according to the record.

75. Project Ninety

You've heard the expression, "going ninety to nothing." Of course, it means going as fast as you possibly can using all the effort you possibly can to hit the maximum you possibly can.

Sometimes churches decline in enrollment. Consequently this affects the attendance and all other facets of a church. *Windy Rich of Nashville created the idea while at Temple Baptist Church and called it "Project Ninety."*

Instead of accepting the ninety days of the summer months as a downhill, slack period, the trend was reversed:

90 days of work
90 workers to go
90 church members enrolled
90 prospects discovered

It sounds like a "one-a-day" workout to solve a problem. The results of the effort were worth the effort. Members were enrolled, prospects were found, attendance was increased, and baptisms resulted.

76. Keeping a Jump Ahead

Louis Bratton, Jr. of Highland Baptist Church in Florence, Alabama used a "jumping frog" for the logo of the fourteen-week summer emphasis. On kickoff Sunday, the pastor led in the main auditorium by signing the first commitment card which indicated, "I will be faithful for ten of the fourteen Sundays." The first Sunday 395 people signed cards. In two weeks, the number "jumped" to 588. Not only was it a commitment to attend but to find prospects, to make contacts, and to do visitation.

People were encouraged if they went on vacation to visit a nearby church and to bring back a bulletin or some type of note indicating they had been present in attendance somewhere in the house of the Lord.

Many promotional signs were used throughout the building in various classes and departments. A high attendance was planned for the last Sunday of the summer with a strong emphasis being made for every class member contacted to be present. The delightful result was 103 more in attendance than the last year.

The overall average was over 53 higher than the previous year. All things did "jump" with the emphasis.

77. Contest of 100s

Bill Tharpe, minister of education of First Baptist Church, Pearland, Texas, gives the following idea to avoid the "summer slump."

1. Purpose of the contest: To avoid the summer slump and to motivate the team of teachers to continue visiting prospects and members for the thirteen weeks of summer.
2. Focus group of participants: Sunday School directors, teachers, and workers.
3. How it worked:
   - It was a contest . . . and publicized as such.
   - Each worker was asked to fill out a card on each Sunday morning, summarizing their outreach activities the previous week.
   - On the card *100 points* were awarded for each of the seven important outreach activities.

- The department director would total the "scores" on the card from his team of workers and send a summary card to the church office with the regular Sunday School records.
- The accumulated total was printed weekly in the newsletter (the church mailout to the home).
- The winning departments in "early" Sunday School and "late" Sunday School were recognized in the morning service following the end of the contest (the church has dual Sunday Schools).
- A banner was awarded to the winning department to display in their room.

The Perfect Summer in Sunday School
"The Contest of 100's"

Department Directors
Weekly Score Card

THIS SCORE CARD IS TO BE FILLED OUT *WEEKLY* BY THE DEPARTMENT DIRECTOR OR DEPARTMENT SECRETARY AND TURNED IN WITH RECORDS ON SUNDAY MORNING.

Please add 100 points for:

_____ 1. *Each new member enrolled in Sunday School*

_____ 2. *Each worker who takes someone (other worker or class member) with them on an outreach opportunity (visitation)*

_____ 3. *Each personal visit made to a prospect*

_____ 4. *Each worker participating in a weekly "outreach opportunity (visitation)*

_____ 5. *Each time a department has 40 percent of its enrollment in attendance on Sunday*

_____ 6. *Each department and/or class which contacts its entire enrollment during the week*

_____ 7. *Each time a department has every worker in attendance during the Sunday session*

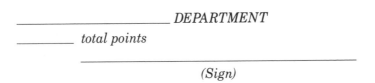

_____ *DEPARTMENT*

_____ *total points*

_____

(Sign)

Bill indicated that the summer over the previous year was an increase in attendance of 257. He attributed it to the fact the contacts were 1,523 more than the previous summer.

New members had not increased as he had hoped since they showed a gain of only nine. However, as he indicated, with the tremendous "exodus" in Texas during that period of time because of the oil crisis, this may have been a tremendous gain.

78. Twin Thermometers

At the beginning of the summer two huge thermometers are made standing side-by-side (use a 4 x 8-foot sheet of celotex or masonite standing on end as the backdrop for two thermometers.) The thermometer on the left represents the total attendance for last summer, and the thermometer on the right represents the thirteen Sundays of the current summer.

Each week, both thermometers are increased according to the total Sunday School attendance of the weeks added together (that is the first three weeks each Sunday's attendance is added to give the total). The thermometers are constructed with red and white ribbon about two inches wide. They are taped together and slipped through two slots on the thermometer at the bottom and the top so they can be moved up each Sunday to show the new total. Each thermometer has thirteen marks on it to represent the weeks.

On the lefthand thermometer, the numbers can be put in ahead of time since last year's record has already been achieved. For example, first Sunday, 150 in attendance; next Sunday, 165; but the total would read 315, and so on at the top of the thermometer. At the top of the thermometer, whatever the total attendance was for all thirteen weeks last year, write the number. For example, it may be 1,869 for the thirteen weeks.

On the righthand thermometer the thirteen marks are placed on the thermometer. Each week a new total is added, using a magic marker or some other instrument to draw the numbers. At the top of the thermometer, the goal was set at the beginning to try and reach more people in attendance than the previous year. For example, the goal for the summer may be 2,000 since the previous summer was 1,869.

During the summer months high emphases are made on attendance, visitation, contacting new members, and prospecting. A number of ideas can be used such as the 10 out of 13 weeks attendance campaign.

Following are testimonies from two churches which used this idea—one a large church and the other a smaller church. *In Salem Baptist Church, Salem, Virginia, Dr. B. Conrad Johnston used the idea with special emphasis on Constant Contact Consciousness during the entire effort.* That is, four different types of contacts—telephone, postcard, seeing someone on the street, or door knocking were encouraged during the summer months.

Their desire was to reach four thousand in attendance by the end of the summer in the thirteen-week period. They were well on their way—in fact ahead—until the hurricane hit one weekend. "The bottom fell out" in attendance that

Sunday, which is understandable. The church also lost its Sunday School director at the beginning of the campaign, and a number of faithful families were transferred out of the community. In spite of that, deleting the one hurricane Sunday, they averaged far beyond anything they'd ever done before.

Let's go to the other side of the country to the Foot Hills Baptist church in Las Vegas, Nevada, where Hoyte Savage is pastor. He used the same concept with the title, "Conquering the summer for Christ," (Rom. 8:37). They have a small Sunday School averaging 35 in attendance. The previous summer they had averaged only 28 per Sunday in attendance. A goal was set to have 500 at the close of the thirteen-week period. This seems like a very ambitious goal for such a small Sunday School. However, when the summer was over, they had a total attendance of 629 with an average attendance of 48 per week.

79. The Hare and the Tortoise

Ed Stephens, Sunday School director for Grace Baptist Church, Warren, Ohio, shares this humorous age-old story idea. Most of us know the figure 20/80, that is, 20 percent of the people do 80 percent of the work while 80 percent of the people do nothing. The secret he worked on was trying to involve more people both inside and outside of his church.

Two wires were strung across the front of the auditorium. On one, a replica of a hare was attached with a simple clothespin, and a replica of a tortoise was hung on the other wire. The church was divided into two groups—the hares and the tortoises. Each week, the winner would receive some type of recognition. Preschool through twelfth grade was one group, and all the adults were in the other group.

At the end of the weeks of emphasis, the losers put on a dinner for the winners, and a "muppet" show was done by the winners (it's easy to see the youth beat the adults). Ed says that two years following the emphasis, people are still talking of the great time and effect it had. People were invited who had not been there before. They had a total of 106 visitors during the emphasis. A number of these people accepted Christ and joined the church in the days that followed. This left people in a receptive mood in attendance and more evangelistic ideas were used. The activities brought the congregation closer together, showing people that Christians can have a good time.

80. Volcano Project

Purpose: Raise Sunday School attendance during "The annual summer slump."

Reason: At First Baptist Church, Powell, Tennessee, the Sunday School attendance throughout the year was about 255. When June would arrive, the bottom dropped out to 210 and stayed like that until school started.

Theme: Twelve signs were placed at strategic locations in halls and on doors. The words on the signs were, *"THE BEST EVER."* The first Sunday of June, the attendance was 215 (fairly traditional). A large poster was placed in the auditorium in the shape of a volcano with a red thermometer-like drawing indicating the thermometer went down into the crater of the volcano. To each side of the volcano were the dates of each of the Sundays with a column for attendance and another column for contacts.

Announcements were made on the opening Sunday about the desires for the entire summer. The goal, obviously, was to have lava flowing constantly over the top.

This was done through contacting. Classes were graded as to active, intermittently active, and dormant, according to the number of contacts they would make. After the initial announcement of the volcano project, the following Sunday the attendance was 230 with 97 contacts. The next Sunday was 233 in attendance with 293 contacts; the third Sunday the attendance was 240 with 310 contacts; the fourth Sunday, 283 with 249 contacts; the fifth Sunday, 301 with 324 contacts. The summer ended with an average of 257 in attendance, whereas the previous year the average attendance had been 215. Two people were baptized, and twelve others joined the church.

Pastor David Patton created the idea.

81. Super Summer Softball

Generally speaking, summer months are looked on as a period when attendance is going to drop. Therefore an attitude of "so we'll just endure it" prevails. This attitude is compounded when the church is pastorless. Many members just give up. *However, this was not the case with Bill Crider who is minister of education at First Baptist Church of Hattiesburg, Mississippi.*

The major emphasis was during the months of June, July, and August. At the close of each month a churchwide fellowship on Sunday night and a "seventh-inning-stretch luncheon" for the two top teams of the league were held. To cap off the month of August there were "playoffs." August 28 was "World Series Day" (high attendance). Baseball uniforms were secured and worn by the four general officers during the "seventh-inning-stretch luncheon" of hotdogs, popcorn, and cokes. Announcements were given in the main auditorium by different people wearing the baseball "garb." Because of special emphases like the above, the fifteen months of "interim blues" were not experienced. Instead, because of the big push throughout the year, especially the summer, the attendance was better than the two previous years. It was jokingly said, "Maybe we do not need a pastor, instead let us find several more outreach directors."

However, when the new pastor arrived, there was no slack to be picked up and things have increased again because of his leadership.

82. Reach Out

The following idea has many flexibilities. It can be used during the summer months. It can be used as a project for the entire year, or it can be used during the fall quarter, whatever the church decides. The idea can be enlarged, or it can be reduced depending on the size of the church.

There are seventeen different categories given for the reach-out emphasis, they are as follows:

Shade Tree Sunday School: Bible study for apartment dwellers. Secure permission to use a community room of an apartment complex or someone's apartment. Invite children, youth, and adults to attend on Sunday mornings. After six months attempt to transfer the class or classes to the regular church location.

Child/reach: Children wear a lapel button that says, "Mom, can I go to Sunday School at _____ Church?" Church kids give their unchurched friends the lapel buttons to wear. The church parents follow through with parents of unchurched children, giving them an invitation to their class.

Sunday Afternoon Outreach: Visit guests who attended

the church (AM) that afternoon. Assignments are made in the conference room after the morning service.

Sunday Lunch Reach Out: Volunteers come to the conference room after morning worship to meet guests and invite them to lunch (at home or to a restaurant).

Entertainment Outreach: Couples or singles invite prospects to their home (or restaurant) for dinner. Cultivate informal friendship.

Continuing Witnessing Training: Thirteen weeks of intensive training on how to share your faith and lead someone to Christ. Meets each Monday evening from 6:30 until 9:00 for study and outreach visitation. Requires memorization (Scripture and model outline), plus a prayer partner.

Partners in Prayer: An organized intercessory prayer ministry. Attend a prayer seminar as a beginning point.

Touch Team: Come to the church once-a-week to read the local newspapers for "people needs." Write notes and letters of congratulation, sympathy, prayerful concern, and so forth. Plants seeds for future ministry.

Morning Reach Out: A weekly time to pray, fellowship, and make outreach visits for shift workers, retirees, ladies who do not work outside their home, and so forth.

Encourager Ministry: Help a new Christian during his/her first few weeks in the faith. Shepherd a new believer.

The Bible Blitz: Deliver free marked New Testaments door-to-door on three or four given Sunday afternoons.

Sunday School Enrollment Blitz: Visit First Baptist Church prospects and encourage them to join the Sunday School. Can be done any time, anywhere people agree to enroll. Follow-up is done by the Sunday School teacher.

Week Day Bible Study: Preset Bible study on the Sermon on The Mount is offered on Thursdays. Other options are possible as interest of leadership increases.

Jail Ministry Witnessing: Sharing your faith with prisoners in the local county jails presently is done on Sunday.

Neighborhood Reach Out: Meet in area homes two to three times a year on a week-day evening. Receive assignments, make visits to prospects in the area, and return for sharing. Save time and gas. Create fellowships useful in newcomer outreach.

Youth Outreach: Various options to contact young people for the church open to youth and adults.

Single Adult Bible Study: A means to involve unenlisted singles in the ministry of the church. Another week-day Bible study opportunity. Enhances fellowship as well.

The above seventeen ideas have worked most effectively for Charles Kuby, who is minister of education/administration at First Baptist Church in Decatur, Alabama.

83. SOS:
Save Our Summer

Obviously this is another SOS idea, but using different words. *Ernie Cecil of Glenwood Baptist Church, Tulsa, Oklahoma, has used this idea effectively.* The signup begins the last week of May and the first week of June through every youth, adult, and children's department. Enough spaces are created on the sign-up sheet for every member in the class. The title of the sheet is, "I'm helping to Save Our Summer. At the bottom of the sheet the person signs the statement: "I plan to be here for Sunday School every Sunday that I'm in town." The goals for each class are as follows:

1. Each Sunday School department will average one more person than the year before.
2. Each department will have two people sign up who will be present on visitation night.

3. Every Sunday School member and visitor will make a commitment to be present for Sunday School every Sunday they are in town during the entire emphasis.

4. Each Sunday School member will be asked to send one card each week to an absentee.

5. All contacters are given *SOS* pens for their efforts in contacting people.

6. During the sign-up campaign all workers and those who have signed will wear stickers saying, "I'm helping save our summer."

7. During one of the months of the emphasis, a contest is held between two groups of Sunday School members divided equally—one led by the pastor and the other led by the minister of youth. In larger churches, this could be the pastor and minister of education, or in smaller churches, this could be the Sunday School director and the pastor. At the end of the month's contest, the winners ate steak and were served by the losers. Another added idea was that the losing leader each Sunday had to SOS (shine the winner's shoes).

8. The SOS was concluded with a high attendance day the last Sunday of August. The emphasis used was: "Be one of the bunch."

Awards were given in the following areas of emphasis:

Most contacts by department
Most contacts by an individual
Highest attendance for a department
Highest total percentage in attendance during the campaign
Department with the highest number of members present
The department with the highest number of people making contacts
Department with the most new members
Department with the most visitors

Department with the most present at Worker's Meeting
Department with the most training awards
Best overall Sunday School department
The highest attendance for a department

The Scripture used for the emphasis was Proverbs 10:5, "He that gathereth in the summer is a wise son."

84. Perfect Attendance

This idea came from Laura Garner, director of third and fourth graders at First Baptist Church, Eldorado, Arkansas. She found this to be very effective. She entitled the emphasis: "Perfect Attendance Chart."

Third and fourth graders work very well when competition with one another is involved. Also, they are encouraged by one another at school for attendance in Sunday School as they see each other.

Record perfect attendance monthly. On the beginning Sunday of a new month, the director announces the children who have had perfect attendance for the previous month. At this time, they receive a scratch-and-sniff sticker of their choice. The attendance chart is an 8½ by 11-inch piece of construction paper that has the names written on to post in the Sunday School Department room.

Teachers also send cards of congratulations to children for their perfect attendance. As children attend each week, they are given a scratch-and-sniff sticker to place by their names.

Presently, Laura is working out a system for those children who come from single-parent homes and can only come 50 percent of the time to church. At the present time, she has 22 enrolled in her third and fourth grade department with an average attendance of fifteen.

Author's note: The Scripture that comes to mind, "Train up a child in the way he should go: and when he is old, he will not depart from it" (Prov. 22:6).

85. Turn on the Green Light

Dr. Mark Hall, assistant pastor of Plainview Baptist Church, Tulsa, Oklahoma, used this idea effectively for his summer-slump campaign.

The campaign is designed to assist a Sunday School is called "Turn on the Green Light." The goal of a campaign is to average as many in attendance during the summer months of June, July, and August as the previous average was in October, November, and December. The reasoning is that churches have growth through the fall and spring, but the summer seems to drop. And the church must spend the fall again regaining where they were in the spring. This campaign is an attempt to stop that slump and allow the fall growth to add to the previous year's growth.

At this writing, Plainview Baptist Church has a Sunday School enrollment of just over 700 with an average attendance of 301. The "payoff" of this particular emphasis is that they maintained an average of 286 during the summer months which is 95 percent of the first six months average.

Make Sunday School workers aware of the program for June, July, and August. Begin the emphasis the first Sunday in June. Erect a green-light board with each department and class having their own lights. The goals are set by averaging the class or department's average attendance beginning in October through April.

Each Sunday class or department members reach their goal, they have a green light lit on the board. Each time they miss their goal, a red light appears. Place the green-light board in the vestibule of the church. Call attention to the progress each Sunday during the Sunday morning service. The pastor, staff member, or Sunday School director should recognize classes and departments reaching their goals.

Since the goal is an average, a point should be made to workers that even if they miss their goal, a week or two weeks, they have the opportunity to make up the difference by having more than their goal the following Sunday. However, the board only reflects each Sunday. It does not show the averages. At the climax of the summer an information sheet showing the averages for the summer can be shared and compared with the previous summer record.

The averages can be distributed during the weekly workers' meeting, by distributing a green-light report listing each class, department, the goals, and the number average. Provide an honor roll of those reaching their goals; those missing it by three or less can be placed in a church paper or bulletin.

8
"Equipping the Saints" Ideas for Growth

86. Sunday School Fundamentals

Doctor Eugene Greer, Jr., program planning director of the Baptist General Convention of Texas, shared with us several excellent lines that give us a view of Sunday School.
"Sunday School meets on Sunday, but Sunday School grows during the week.
"Sunday School is full-time.

It meets on Sunday, ministers every day of the week, trains on Wednesday, parties on holidays and Fridays, enlists at all hours of the night and day, and wins people to Christ as opportunities come. Yes, Sunday School is full-time."

Gene offered some words he heard Mack Douglas, former pastor of Tower Grove Baptist Church in Saint Louis, say concerning stewardship:

"Nearly every dollar that goes into the church offering plate was brought to church in the pocket of someone attending Sunday School."

The complimentary close of Gene's letter was a powerful statement: "Yours is the conviction that Sunday done right IS the main thing."

87. On-the-Job Training

T.D. McCulloch of Texarkana, Texas, has used this idea in a number of churches he served as minister of education.

On recommendation of all of his adult teachers and department leadership, T.D. asked them to select potential workers from their members. He composed a list of names from all the suggestions, then he put these names on another sheet of paper. He handed them back to the workers and asked them to select a person to be their trainee.

The trainee observed, helped, and studied the age-group book and attended workers' meetings and visited with the trainer for four to six months. Once a month, a staff member or coordinator conducted a special monthly session to supplement some of the teaching of the work of the trainer.

T.D. indicated this prepared people to be available literally in just a few weeks. Some people take a little longer to be used elsewhere in the organization. Using this concept while at Travis Avenue in Fort Worth, T.D. trained workers and staffed the youth division. At East Grand in Dallas, he used this idea to fill vacancies and enlarge the total organization. At Beaumont in Texarkana, he was able to create the dual Sunday Schools and to extend it to the satellite Sunday School. This gave him a constant flow of good workers.

The advantage of this idea and concept is that people are able to work in a particular area to discover whether or not they are best suited emotionally and physically before a final commitment is made to an age group. It also allows a trainee to progress at their own rate of learning.

88. "SSALT": Sunday School and Leadership Training

SSALT is the name for a church's potential teacher training program. The name SSALT is an acronym for *S*unday *S*chool *a*nd *L*eadership *T*raining. "Ye are the salt of the earth" (Matt. 5:13). This verse gives an effective handle on the program for promotion and emphasis. It has a little more "umph" to it than using the simple phrase of potential teacher training. *Joseph Borgkvist, Sr., minister of education, First Baptist Church, West Columbia, South Carolina, gave us this idea* and said it's best to have eight to twelve in a class because it gives it a realistic setting to an average adult-size class which has an enrollment of about twenty to twenty-five. The class meets during the Sunday School hour to ensure better attendance and eliminate those presently teaching or serving in the Sunday School organization. This also makes everyone in the class feel less reluctant to participate since they are all on an equal footing more or less. The fifteen-week length is selected in order to give participants enough class time to earn credits for three study course books toward their Sunday School leadership diploma.

Any type of teacher/leadership training material can be used in the program, plus the basic books. The material used is a mixture of information and methods along with basic material coming from the Church Study Course books required for the Sunday School Leadership diplomas. The objective is to train potential Sunday School leaders in the foundational elements of Sunday School work as a whole, not just in teaching methods. The following is an outline of the course:

Week 1. Introduction, overview, and Sunday School organization

Week 2. How to study the Bible (basics of interpretation)

Week 3. Basic teaching tools (materials available)

Week 4. Basic Sunday School work (adult).

Week 5. Basic Sunday School work (adult emphasis).

Week 6. Bible teaching for adults through the Sunday School.

Week 7. Bible teaching for adults through the Sunday School.

Week 8. Creative teaching methods (five basic methods every teacher should know and master: lecture, case study, buzz groups, brainstorming, and discussion).

Week 9. Understanding today's adults.

Week 10. Understanding today's adults.

Week 11. Doctrine (overview of basics).

Week 12. Doctrine (overview of basics).

Week 13. Practice teaching.

Week 14. Evaluation of practice teaching.

Week 15. Outreach and evangelism through the Sunday School organization.

Joe indicated that SSALT as a handle for the name of the class can give some real significance to what leaders attempt to accomplish. He indicated a number of Scripture verses that refer to "salt" plus the various uses of salt as a mineral substance.

A number of applications can be used with the word *salt* in illustrations. Salt is used to flavor and to make food taste better. Christian leaders are to flavor the world and make it a better place. Salt is used to preserve foods. Christian leaders are to help believers grow and preserve them until Christ returns. Salt can be used as a healing agent. Christian leaders are to be healers of the lost and downtrodden. Salt can be used to draw moisture. Christian leaders are to bring nonbelievers and believers to Christ. It is easy to see other applications that can also be made with regard to qualities desired in Christian leaders.

A number of phrases can be used to promote teacher/leader training with the term *salt* such as: "Spice up your teaching with salt," or "A little salt can really flavor and add to your teaching class." Another is, "Have you salted your teaching?" And, "You can be the salt of the earth for your class." As one can see, a number of phrases can be used. Also, ask the people involved in the class how they can come up with some promotional ideas and do a little creative brainstorming.

89. A Spiritual Charge to Sunday School Workers

Many Sunday School leaders are constantly looking for passages of Scripture and words that emphasize all the duties and characteristics of a worker in Sunday School or for the total organization. *Charles Keller, director of missions in Auburn, California, gave us the following:*

(1) Be faithful (1 Cor. 4:2).
(2) Be a steward (Mal. 3:10).
(3) Be Bible-centered (Ps. 119:16).
(4) Be a planner (Luke 14:28).
(5) Be a student (Prov. 15:28).
(6) Be a team player (1 Cor. 10:9).
(7) Be loyal (Heb. 10:25).
(8) Be a witness (Prov. 11:30).
(9) Be in prayer (1 Thess. 5:17).
(10) Be a doer (Jas. 1:27).
(11) Be worthy (Eph. 4:1-3).
(12) Be a minister (Acts 2:46).

90. New Year's Celebration

First Baptist Church, Forest City, Arkansas, began their new Sunday School year in a unique fashion. On October 2, the Sunday School members met by departments in the main worship center ten minutes before the Sunday School hour started. The members were led in a chorus of "Get All Excited." They were challenged by the minister of education, and a prayer of commitment and commission was given by the pastor. Next, the members were led in singing "Victory in Jesus," as they closed the old Sunday School year and began the new.

Commitments were made by the workers. Appreciation was expressed for a tremendous job the previous year. In the midst of the singing, a bell was rung at the time of the beginning of the new Sunday School hour. People began to rejoice with "Happy New Year, Happy New Year" and "God loves you, God loves you." At the close of the chorus of "Victory in Jesus," the members were dismissed to go to their new classes. The church had adopted a challenge for the coming year of "Helping people know Jesus" with an exciting Sunday School as the primary force.

Thanks, Don Matthews, minister of education and Delton Beall, pastor.

91. Outreach to People Who Are Different

It was Wednesday night prayer service, and the preacher was talking about the needs in the church family. He completed his list and made the "mistake" of saying, "Is there anything any of you have to add?"

Joy, my handicapped friend, was seated beside me (Lynne Scott) flipping through the books she had checked out from the church library. Teaching her to check out books according to the rules had been a summer project—Joy raised her hand.

"Yes, ma'am," came the calm acknowledgement of the pastor.

"I just want you to know that I brought my books back," she stated firmly and loudly. "And I checked out two more. I'm going to read them and bring them back next week."

Even through my embarrassment I was aware of people trying to find ways to look at us.

The pastor responded, "That's just fine."

Without a moment's hesitation, Joy looked up at him with the simplicity of childhood and said, "You sweet thing."

Grinning, the preacher said, "I wish you'd tell my wife."

"Well, where is she?" Joy started looking around the church.

Bringing a mentally and emotionally handicapped person into the total experience of the church family has greatly enriched my life and understanding of the healing power of the church—the body of Christ.

Joy had been institutionalized much of her life. Her history showed a 36-year-old woman with potential but who had never learned to live in relationship with other people in an acceptable way. Opportunities for some "normal" friends would help her to develop social skills and a wholeness of being that might allow her to find a place in the world that would accept her. Touched by the thought of this woman and her struggle with life, I wondered if one relationship would offer that kind of healing. What would it mean to her life if she were brought into contact with a whole, healing community of accepting persons?

One ministry in the church is for handicapped persons: the mentally retarded ministry is an activity that involves helping the family cope with their difficult situation and provides a special class designed to meet the retarded person's unique needs.

This is essential. The idea involved in this concept is to provide social and intellectual contact that might give these people the opportunity to develop to their own creative potential.

With these thoughts in mind, I began the process of involving Joy in the life of the church family. Some initial contacts were necessary. I was excited and anxious about my vision when I made an appointment to visit with my pastor, Dr. Joe Lovelady, on a Friday morning. I found my discussion with the pastor to be a most helpful experience. He brought my thinking back to the reality of who I was working with—the local church, a volunteer organization. The process of implementing any special project depends on a person as catalyst.

Together we worked out a plan which I would share with the church during our "prayer-and-praise" time the following Sunday night. This plan involved bringing Joy with me to the Wednesday night supper and allowing her to have contact with the total church family, having her participate as a teacher's helper in the fourth through sixth grade GA group. This gave her a small-group encounter in intellectual growth and an invitation to the church family to relate themselves to Joy and myself in anyway they might feel was natural for them.

Through this encounter with my pastor, I learned the value of having an idea, talking it over with the people who might be involved, and shaping a plan to include the unique qualities of those who will be involved. Visions are great fun, but the real meaning, fulfillment, and creativity come through working out the vision in relationship with others.

Sunday night, a shy, frightened person told the church family about a young mentally retarded woman with whom I would be working. I told them about her family's struggle to provide for their daughter's needs. I told them of Joy's needs for friends who would accept and talk with her. I was uncomfortable about my emotional appeal, but the response was positive. Five people came and volunteered to help by having Joy and me come to their homes. One young woman, the minister of youth's wife, wanted to have a special Sunday School time with Joy. There was concern and curiosity. People were interested. They affirmed my belief that as we give prayer requests, we can present requests that require human action and find people who will respond.

On Wednesday night, I met with the GA group. We sat on the floor and talked about people who were different. It was a challenge to find words that would communicate new dimensions to the word *retarded* and establish a bond with the girls that would help them feel and understand Joy's needs and what the GA group had that would help meet those needs. I talked about the differences—her age, her physical appearance, her slow speech, and her inability to learn quickly. I talked about her need for friends and how they could help her learn, simply by allowing her to be in the group. The girls were great—warm, accepting, curious, and willing to try.

The individual difference our church family made became apparent quickly. I admit, initially, I lived in fear of the possibility of her impulsive nature when she came with me to church. However, I began to see that even though people were insecure at times around Joy, there was a basic acceptance and a genuine love for her. Joy never missed an opportunity to be involved. When the cards for the sick were passed around during Wednesday night prayer service, she signed them in huge block letters, signing her name, my name, my mother's name, and her father's name. When we left the service early one night, she turned and waved good-bye to the pastor.

Joy began to watch the Sunday morning TV show. She called the prayer line and asked for prayer for her family. Joy learned the verses from her special Bible class and shared these with people outside the church. The most significant part of this involvement was that Joy felt loved by a group of people and found a place where she could be herself and still have opportunities to grow and to change.

Much was learned from this experience. I discovered there is a place in the church for every kind of ministry. The creative potential is there within God's people. The programs do not bind us to a structure that does not provide for something or someone who is different. The ministry possibilities are present with the relationship between people and the church family. There is much potential among God's people. The power of God's Spirit makes the church dynamic with life-giving people, gifts, and the wisdom to meet human needs.

"Joy had gained faith beyond my expectations," admitted Lynne Scott, counselor of First Baptist Church, Newnan, Georgia.

We arrived early at church for Joy's regular Sunday

night session. The teacher was late. I was tired. Joy was excited. I was angry. Joy was sensitive.

"You look down as anything," she said looking with me with those huge searching eyes.

"I'm not, just thinking."

"Oh? Those eyes of yours watch me just like Jesus. Oh, I missed you so much," she said.

"When? I haven't been gone that long."

"This weekend I prayed, please Jesus, take care of her. You bring her back to me. If anything had happened to you, my heart would be broken," she said watching me very carefully.

"Well, Jesus does take are of me," I said.

"I know He does," she responded. "Jesus is always with us. He's everywhere. He's right here. He's right there beside you," she said as she pointed to the air beside me. "Why don't you talk with Him?"

She got up and walked over beside me, pointed her finger again. "There He is, right there!"

"I do talk with Him, Joy. I pray every day." I was faltering, I knew. It was as if she saw Him, and I could not.

92. Strengthen Content
Teaching—Recall/Retention/Reliving

It is difficult for youth and adult class members to remember the content of a Sunday School lesson after several weeks. Some members have difficulty remembering last week.

To help members retain and recall previous lesson content, the following growth idea works wonders.

Take three to four layers of heavy table cover paper that

is used in the fellowship hall for suppers and banquets. Most rolls of paper are 48 inches wide. Therefore, tear sheets that are four feet by five feet. Mount the three or four sheets on top of each other. This prevents ink bleedthrough onto a wall Attach to a wall in the classroom behind or to one side of the teacher.

At the close of the class period (stop about five minutes early) give each member a crayon or marking pen to write a simple phrase or sentence about what they received from the day's lesson. Write the statement large enough for all to see from their chair in the classroom. Ask them to put their initial by their written thought.

With the paper behind the teacher, the pupil will have the tendency to look at what he wrote the week before or several weeks before. He will mentally weigh his state-ment—and others. They will once again rethink their thought or the thought of someone else. Remember the statement—"Repetition aids to learning."

Most Sunday School lessons emphasize a theme for sev-eral weeks—sometimes the entire quarter. Using the above method causes reflection, repetition of thoughts, new con-siderations, ideas, and enlightening the impressions of others.

The final analysis—recall/retention/reliving—three ba-sics of long-term memory take place. Better teaching is ac-complished.

9
Worker Appreciation Ideas for Growth

93. Appreciation Banquet

Every person likes to hear his or her name called in public and especially loves to be recognized for accomplishments. Because of this fact, worker appreciation banquets are a must in every church regardless of size. A well-planned banquet will accentuate the positive and can do more to motivate workers than one realizes. Several important factors to keep in mind when planning the banquet are theme, promotion, recognition, program, and special arrangements.

Choose a *theme* to plan the banquet around. *Cecil H. Reid, Jr., minister of education at Huffman Baptist Church, Birmingham, Alabama, used the theme: "You are the apple of our eyes."* The slogan was printed on a huge banner and hung on the wall behind the speaker's table. All decorations centered around the apple—a universal object for teacher appreciation. Each person took home a beautiful, delicious red apple as a token of appreciation.

Promotion is essential and should start a month before the banquet takes place. Every worker receives a personal invitation in the mail with a response slip to be filled out and returned for a reservation. All workers are honored guests. The banquet is promoted for the entire month.

Recognition of workers is important! The purpose of having the banquet is to recognize and honor people. Standard recognition needs to be made such as, diplomas earned, standard units, enrollment goals reached, attendance, and so forth. Consider recognizing each department for some area of outstanding ministry. Encourage the Sunday School council to do this since they know the people best. Be creative in recognition. Above all be positive.

In some departments it may be difficult to think of a good way to recognize them because they may not be "up to par." You may have to come up with some category such as: "Great Cooperative Spirit," "All Workers Always on Time," and "Best Preschool Room Organization." Again, create a positive mind-set among the workers. Hopefully, the following year through positive efforts will bring them to lead and excel in areas such as enrollment gained, diplomas earned, standard achievement, and other major emphases of the Sunday School.

Recognize special groups like nursery workers and greeters who do great work but many times go unnoticed. Cecil Reed presents a special gift to every council member as an expression of the church's appreciation for a job well done. All recognitions took approximately 30 minutes but were worth every second.

Once you get the people there, have a good *program* planned for them. The banquet was started at 5:30 PM with a "happy hour" (appetizers in another room other than where the banquet was prepared). This gives a time of fellowship with the supper beginning at 6:00 PM. The banquet meal was served for just a slight cost higher than the regular Wednesday night suppers. By the way, the appreciation banquet was held on Wednesday night. This seemed to work much better when more folks were accustomed to coming to church, and other people could break loose and be there.

Immediately following the recognition, special music was provided that set the stage for the special guest speaker (the author was the special guest speaker). The pastor made a few closing remarks, prayed, and sent the people happily on their way. From "happy hour" to the benediction took two hours. My part of the program was 45 minutes and flew by quickly.

Special arrangements were made in several key areas that added to the success. The older youth who were not workers kept the preschoolers and provided special activities for first through sixth grades and helped serve the tables. This allowed all workers to attend the banquet. It enabled all parents to enjoy the evening without worrying about their children. Three hundred and thirty adults attended the banquet, 85 children, and 25 preschoolers, giving a total of 440 for the evening. Cecil's attitude and remarks were, "We really appreciate our workers for they are the apples of our eyes."

94. I Appreciate My Sunday School Teacher

George Humphreys, Sunday School director of Gardenside Baptist Church, Lexington, Kentucky, shared this appreciation idea. The Sunday School director chose a person from each class to collect comments from as many class members as possible and had them tell why they appreciated their teacher. This was started four weeks prior to teacher appreciation day. Each person was given a pastel-colored 3- by 5-inch card and was asked to write comments of appreciation for their teacher on the cards. The cards were then returned and mounted on black construction paper with the small, gummed corner tabs used in mounting photographs in an album—one card per page.

The pages were then placed in an attractive folder with a label on the cover of each folder. The label read: "I appreciate my Sunday School teacher (name of teacher and date).

On teacher appreciation day, the classes presented the folders to their teachers.

Author's note: These presentations could be done in the class, department, main auditorium, or at a banquet. The idea is excellent. Adapt it according to your congregation.

95. Letters of Appreciation

From time to time, it is good for a Sunday School director, pastor, or minister of education to write personal letters to the workers. It is not always necessary to wait for some great occasion to take place. (Many people do not have great events that are tremendously recognizable except being present Sunday after Sunday School in faithfulness, and giving the best they're capable of giving.) From time to time, words of appreciation, a pat on the back, and "Well done, thou good and faithful servant" need to be given.

Following is a sample letter the minister of education at Two Rivers Baptist Church in Nashville sent to me.

Dear Neil:

Someone has wisely suggested there are four types of people in any organization, including the church. There are those who make things happen, those who watch things happen, those who try to keep things from happening, and those who do not even know anything is happening.

It is obvious to me you are in the group God uses to make things happen. The skills God has given you, and your willingness to use them for His glory, give us a positive means to affect Two Rivers for the cause of Christ.

No one really knows the lasting and powerful influence of a life like yours, nor do we really know how to say how much we appreciate what you are doing. You are an important part of the team God has given. Thank you for all you are doing at Two Rivers. You've blessed my life and many more.

My prayer is that this Sunday School year at Two Rivers will be its finest.

Because He lives,
Ray E. Moss, Minister of Administration Education

96. We Appreciate You

Roselyn Toliver, outreach director of St. Stephen's Baptist Church, La Puenta, California, gave us the following recognition idea.

A special recognition day is set for all Sunday School workers. They are asked to sit in a special area of the sanctuary for the 11 AM service. Each worker wears a ribbon of identification on his/her garment during Sunday School. The words on the ribbon read: "We appreciate you." This recognizes the workers during Sunday School, through the preaching hour, and all through the rest of the day.

The pastor will lead in a commitment prayer for all the workers, using special readings from the Word of God.

A uniqueness during the invitation is to give not only the workers an opportunity of total commitment of their life to the Lord and for the Sunday School, but also an invitation to all the people not enrolled in Sunday School to enroll right then and there. They are urged to put the cards in an offering plate on the Lord's Supper table.

There were thirty-two enrolled on that special Sunday.

97. February: Love Month

February is an excellent time to show people we appreciate them. However, sometimes all we do is appreciate the workers and leave out other people who are doing an effective job in the Sunday School class. *Kenneth Kyker, pastor of the Antioch Baptist Church in Johnson City, Tennessee, used this approach to show appreciation to workers in the Sunday School classes.*

The emphasis was made on "Love Your Teacher." A grocery store furnished apples for every teacher in the Sunday School. On February 14, the emphasis was, "Bring someone you love and care for." A restaurant furnished six free tickets for a steak dinner to the leaders of the winning class, teacher, outreach evangelism leader, and four care group leaders. On the twenty-first, the emphasis was, "Love our outreach leader." Carnations were given to each outreach leader of the Sunday School. (Incidentally, they got double use out of the carnations because they were used as decorations for the churchwide Valentine banquet.) On the twenty-eighth, the emphasis was, "Love your care leader." A yardstick with the motto, "Gather the people" was given to each care leader. After the emphasis was over, a surprise happened. The highest attendance in February was reached. Turn February to a love month.

98. Member Appreciation Day

"MAD Sunday" is an acronym for Member Appreciation Day. It is a high attendance day for Sunday School. Start preparation four to six weeks before MAD Sunday. This can be either a fall or a spring emphasis. Use the following steps.

(1) Set the goal. It could be one more than the enrollment or one more than ever before in the class.

(2) Get all class members to sign commitment slips and turn them in as soon as possible.

(3) When commitment slips are turned in, place the names on the commitment chart, then turn the commitment slips over to the Sunday School director. He will report to the church how many are committed each Sunday.

(4) Appoint a telephone committee. The committee telephones class members two weeks before MAD Sunday to see if they have signed commitment slips and encouraged them to be present. Each member should be telephoned, on the Saturday before MAD Sunday, by the teacher or outreach leader to remind them of the day.

(5) Each person in the Sunday School class is assigned at least one other person to visit. Make sure every member and prospect is visited during the period of emphasis.

(6) Encourage every one to attend regular worship services every Sunday.

(7) Enroll every new person if possible.

(8) Follow through with telephone and personal visitation. Mail cards and letters to absentees.

(9) On that day, the class that reaches its goal will be recognized during the worship service.

(10) Keep in mind it will take hard work, but the goal can be reached.

(11) Saturate everything you do with prayer.

(12) Invite the lost to attend Sunday School. They are easier to reach for Christ by being in Bible study.

(13) Invite every church member not enrolled in Sunday School to be a part of the day.

(14) Make posters and have them posted throughout the church as a reminder of member appreciation day. A poster contest could encourage creativity.

(15) A commitment chart should be placed in every teaching area.

(16) Promote the event from the pulpit weekly during the worship service.

(17) During the worship services on the special day recognize Sunday School members and leaders for doing an excellent job. Read the results that have been accomplished during the period of emphasis—new members enrolled, total number of contacts, high attendance, names of the classes which reached their goals during the campaign.

(18) During the day in the main auditorium, enrollment slips and cards should be given out for visitors and church members to be enrolled in Sunday School.

J. Billy Brown, growth consultant of the Georgia Baptist Convention, used this idea in a number of his pastorates. He indicated this could be done each Sunday during a campaign of enrolling new people in the main auditorium.

99. Highlighting the Worker

Mark Cordrey, minister of education of Meadow Wood Baptist Church of Midwest City, Oklahoma, says, "We highlight on classes and departments each week from one of the four sections of the Sunday School, preschool, children, youth, or adults. In the article we mention the age group, the Sunday School hour of 8:15 or 11:00 and the names of the workers in the class. We tell either about their growth, their special events, their efforts, their teaching series, and what they are learning; or general information that draws attention to the special teaching unit." Some of the benefits of using the spotlight on the Sunday School are:

Increased awareness of what is going on in the different ares of the Sunday School.

Motivation of workers by seeing their name in writing.

Telling of needs in different areas of the Sunday School.

Training through informing the church of what the Sunday School is all about in different areas.

General information of Sunday School work and many other opportunities can be mentioned.

This highlights the work of the Sunday School and at the same time gives recognition to those people doing a job.

Mark indicated this methodology is especially helpful when they do their high attendance Sunday once a quarter. There is nothing like letting the "light" shine.

100. The Golden Key Award

Present a "Golden Key Award" to the person with the greatest contribution to Bible study for the month or quarter. The award could be a walnut plaque with an engraved brass plate, a well-lettered poster, or a printed certificate. The areas of emphasis could be the following:

Contacts: Recognize the person reporting the greatest number of contacts. This would include personal visits (door knocking), phone calls, postcards, or contacting people as they go about daily activities.

Enrollment: Enrolling the highest number of people in Sunday School in one month is another area that can be emphasized. Using the open enrollment concept allows a person to enroll people outside of the class or department. It allows a person to enroll people into other classes or departments, especially into Homebound and Cradle Roll departments. Persons doing the enrolling need to sign their names on the enrollment card.

Training: Emphasis could be placed on special study courses. Recognize the person earning the greatest number of awards in a given quarter. I did this for a year at First Baptist Church, New Orleans. Over 2,500 awards were earned. One person earned sixty-five and another earned sixty-four awards.

Contributors

Donald G. Allen
Exchange Avenue Baptist
   Church
1312 South Pennsylvania
Oklahoma City, OK 73108

Dick Baker
First Baptist Church
P.O. Box 66
Duluth, GA 30136

Gary Ball
Friendship Baptist Church
Coon Rapids, MN

Joseph Borgkvist, Jr.
First Baptist Church
400 State Street
West Columbia, SC 29169

Lewis E. Bratton
Highland Baptist Church
219 Simpson Street
Florence, AL 35630

J. Billy Brown
Georgia Baptist Convention
Sunday School Department
2930 Flowers Road, South
Atlanta, GA 30341

W. R. Bumpas
Wilshire Baptist Church
6314 Rincon Way
Dallas, TX 75214

Phil Burgman
First Baptist Church
7419 North 58th Avenue
Glendale, AZ 85301

Odell Carpenter
First Baptist Church
P.O. Box 68
114 East Breckenridge Avenue
Bixby, OK 74008

Logan Carlisle
Bethlehem Baptist Church
Clarksville, GA 30523

Ernie Cecil
5400 Charles Page Boulevard
Tulsa, OK 74127

Mary Clayton
First Baptist Church
2708 Evans Drive
Durham NC 27705

Mark D. Cordray
Meadowood Baptist Church
2816 Woodcrest
Midwest City, OK 73110

Jimmy Cox
Rosedale Baptist Church
Abingdon, VA

Bill Crider
First Baptist Church
510 West Pine Street
Hattiesburg, MS 39401

Carol Deel
Olivet Baptist Church
1775 South Beretania Street
Honolulu, HI 96826

J. A. Eddington
Sequoyah Hills Baptist Church
714 North Harvard
Tulsa, OK 74115

Mike Felder
St. Simons Baptist Church
729 Ocean Boulevard
St. Simons Island, GA 31522

Charles Fox
Heritage Baptist Church
Annapolis, MD

Carey Froelich
University Baptist Church
304 Leeward Drive
Baton Rouge, LA 70808

Bob Fuston
Baptist General Convention
   of Texas
333 North Washington
Dallas, TX 75246-1798

Laura Garner
First Baptist Church
200 West Main Street
Eldorado, AR 71730

Tim Gentry
West Roseville Baptist Church
P.O. Box 926
Roseville, CA 95661

E. Eugene Greer, Jr.
Baptist General Convention
   of Texas
State Missions Commission
333 North Washington
Dallas, TX 75246-1798

Mark E. Hall
Plainview Baptist Church
1330 S 119 E Avenue
Tulsa, OK 74128

James E. Harvey
First Baptist Church
317 Sheffield Place
Franklin, TN 37064

Sam Hendry
Immanuel Baptist Church
1101 East Main
Shawnee, OK 74801

Jeff Hicks
Gardenside Baptist Church
1667 Alexandria Drive
Lexington, KY 40504-2198

Wanda B. Hicks
First Baptist Church
6 Northfield Road
Signal Mountain, TN 37377

Sid Hopkins
Lawrenceville Baptist
   Association
1648 Highway 29 South
Lawrenceville, GA 30244

Russell Houser
First Baptist Church

P.O. Box 404
Wakita, OK 73771

Don Hull
Fielder Road Baptist Church
2011 South Fielder Road
Arlington, TX 76013

George Humphrey
Gardenside Baptist Church
1667 Alexandria Drive
Lexington, KY 40504

Neil E. Jackson, Jr.
Baptist Sunday School Board
127 9th Avenue, North
Nashville, TN 37234

Gary L. Johnson
Vale Baptist Church
811 South Vale Street
Bloomington, IL 61701

Jack Johnson
Arizona Baptist Convention
Suite 112
400 West Camelback Road
Phoenix, AZ 85013

B. Conrad Johnston
Salem Baptist Church
Salem, Virginia

Charles A. Kellar
Feather River & Sierra
  Foothills Associations
420 7th Street
Lincoln, CA 95648

Ronald K. Kinzel, Sr.
First Baptist Church

P.O. Box 241
Highway 122
McDowell, KY 41647

Carl Kuby
First Baptist Church
P.O. Box 326
Decatur, AL 35602

Kenneth Kyker
Antioch Baptist Church
1014 Antioch Road
Johnson City, TN 37604

Rita Loadholt
First Baptist Church
Roswell, GA

Don R. Matthews
First Baptist Church
507 North Rosser
Forrest City, AR 72335

T. D. McCulloch
3015 Moores Lane
Texarkana, TX 75503

Kay Moebes
Shades Mountain Baptist
  Church
2017 Columbiana Road
Birmingham, AL 35226

Verlon W. Moore
Hilldale Baptist Church
2001 Madison
Clarksville, TN 37043

L. L. Morriss
Pastor Emeritus
First Baptist Church
Midland, TX

Ray Moss
Two Rivers Baptist Church
2800 McGavock Pike
Nashville, TN 37214

Robert Lynn Park
Fayetteville First Baptist
  Church
205 East Stonewall Avenue
Fayetteville, GA 30214

David Patton
Powell First Baptist
P.O. Box 12218
Knoxville, TN 37912

Bo Prosser
First Baptist Church
710 Mimosa Boulevard
Roswell, GA 30075

Walter Rarrick
First Baptist Church
525 South Avenue
Springfield, MO 65806

J. W. Ray
First Baptist Church
Rattan, OK 75462

Cecil H. Reid, Jr.
Huffman Baptist Church
700 Huffman Road
Birmingham, AL 35215

Windy Rich
304 Edgeview Drive
Nashville, TN 37211

Michael S. Sabo
Bayshore Baptist Church

701 San Jacinto
La Porte, TX 77571

Hoyte Savage
Foot Hills Baptist Church
Las Vegas, NV

Lynne D. Scott
First Baptist Church
115 West Washington
Newnan, GA 30264

Ronald G. Skaggs
First Baptist Church
111 South Seventh
Muskogee, OK 74401

Edward C. Smith, Jr.
Northside Park Baptist Church
1877 Howell Mill Road, NW
Atlanta, GA 30318

Gary Stanton
Midwestern Baptist Theological
  Seminary
Box 22
5001 North Oak TR Freeway
Kansas City, MO 64118

Ed Stephens
Central Baptist Church
1301 North Road
Niles, OH 44446

Tommy Stevens
Allen Baptist Church
Route 6, Box 114, Belle
  Highway
Brownsville, TN 38012

Charles Stone, Jr.
Greater Gwinnett Baptist
   Church
1410 Old Peach Tree Road
Suwanne, GA 30174

Bill Tharp
First Baptist Church
4201 West Broadway
Pearland, TX 77581

Glenn Thompson
Sharon Baptist Church
Wichita, KS

Roselyn Toliver
St. Stephen's Baptist Church
1720 Walnut
La Puente, CA

Charles Westbrook
East Bay Missionary Baptist
6610 Simmons Lane
Riverview, FL 33569

Ron Wilcoxson
Brickwood Baptist Church
205 Homecrest
Kennett, MO 63857